VOLLEYBALL

Steps to Success

Second Edition

Barbara L. Viera, MS
Bonnie Jill Ferguson, MS
University of Delaware, Newark

Human Kinetics

Library of Congress Cataloging-in-Publication Data

Viera, Barbara L., 1941-
  Volleyball : steps to success / Barbara L. Viera, Bonnie Jill
Ferguson.--2nd ed.
    p.   cm. -- (Steps to success activity series)
  Includes bibliographical references.
  ISBN 0-87322-646-1
    1. Volleyball.   I. Ferguson, Bonnie Jill, 1957-   II. Title.
  III. Series.
  GV1015.3.V54   1996
  796.325--dc20

                                    95-42643
                                      CIP

ISBN: 0-87322-646-1

Copyright © 1996 Human Kinetics Publishers, Inc.
Copyright © 1989 by Leisure Press

Series and Developmental Editor: Judy Patterson Wright, PhD; **Assistant Editor:** John Wentworth; **Editorial Assistant:** Jennifer Hemphill; **Copyeditor:** Bob Replinger; **Proofreader:** Jim Burns; **Typesetter:** Kathy Boudreau-Fuoss; **Text Designer:** Keith Blomberg; **Layout Artist:** Denise Lowry; **Cover Designer:** Jack Davis; **Photographer (cover):** Wilmer Zehr; **Illustrator:** Sharon Barner; **Mac Artist:** Studio 2D; **Printer:** United Graphics

Instructional Designer for the Steps to Success Activity Series: Joan N. Vickers, EdD, University of Calgary, Calgary, Alberta, Canada

Human Kinetics books are available at special discounts for bulk purchase. Special editions or book excerpts can also be created to specification. For details, contact the Special Sales Manager at Human Kinetics.

Printed in the United States of America   10 9 8

Human Kinetics
Web site: www.HumanKinetics.com

United States: Human Kinetics
P.O. Box 5076
Champaign, IL 61825-5076
800-747-4457
e-mail: humank@hkusa.com

Canada: Human Kinetics
475 Devonshire Road, Unit 100
Windsor, ON N8Y 2L5
800-465-7301 (in Canada only)
e-mail: orders@hkcanada.com

Europe: Human Kinetics
107 Bradford Road
Stanningley
Leeds LS28 6AT, United Kingdom
+44 (0)113 255 5665
e-mail: hk@hkeurope.com

Australia: Human Kinetics
57A Price Avenue
Lower Mitcham, South Australia 5062
08 8277 1555
e-mail: liahka@senet.com.au

New Zealand: Human Kinetics
P.O. Box 105-231, Auckland Central
09-523-3462
e-mail: hkp@ihug.co.nz

CONTENTS

PREFACE

Although volleyball was invented in the United States, not until recently has our country assumed a leadership role in its development. As is true in most sports, the key to player development is learning correct technique early on. This second edition of *Volleyball: Steps to Success* has 12 steps that introduce you to the game of volleyball and its skills and strategies. The book can be successfully used by beginning players wanting to learn the game, by intermediate players attempting to improve their skills, and by teachers and coaches as a reference. As a beginning player, you will improve your skills more quickly by understanding the correct method of performance and why each skill is important in a competitive setting. Intermediate players will find the "Success Stoppers" section in each step helpful in analyzing their performance errors and discovering how to correct them. Teachers and coaches can use the book to find ideas for drills and teaching progressions.

The unique step-by-step format allows for logical progression while providing competitive activities and 99 challenging drills. Suggested ways to increase or decrease the difficulty level of the drills lets you progress at your pace as you practice the skills within drills that closely simulate game situations. While you practice the basic skills, you'll learn not only the key phrases and concepts for correct performance, but also when to use them.

The sequence of the 12 steps is not random. It has been carefully developed over our long playing, teaching, and coaching careers. The 12 steps are organized from the simpler to the more complex skills. They are also sequenced similarly to the order that skills would be performed in a competitive situation. Thus, as each skill is learned and practiced, it can be added to the sequence, which eventually allows a competitive rally. This sequence—the forearm pass of the serve to the setter, the set, the attack, and the block or dig to begin the sequence again in transition—is repeated continuously in a game situation. As you improve your level of performance, you'll enjoy the game more and more!

As in any project of this magnitude, many people have contributed to its successful completion. We would like to thank Karen Woodie for her help with word processing and computer technology; David Barlow, PhD, for his help in the filming presented to the artist for sketching diagrams; and our subjects, Jeanne Dyson Scott, Nancy Griskowitz, Maggie Hennigan, Sue Stauffer, Pat Castagno, John Aiello, and Clare Farrall. We would also like to extend our sincere appreciation to Sharon Barner and Studio 2D, who transformed photos and diagrams into expert drawings.

THE STEPS TO SUCCESS STAIRCASE

Get ready to climb a staircase—one that will lead you to be a great volleyball player. You cannot leap to the top; you get there by climbing one step at a time.

Each of the 12 steps you are about to take is an easy transition from the one before. The first few steps of the staircase provide a foundation—a solid foundation of basic skills and concepts. As you progress, you will learn how to connect groups of those seemingly isolated skills. Practicing common combinations of volleyball skills will give you the experience you need to begin making natural and accurate decisions on the court. You will learn to make the right moves in various game situations—whether you're serving or receiving, spiking or blocking. As you near the top of the staircase, the climb will ease, and you'll find that you have developed a sense of confidence in your volleyball playing ability that makes further progress a real joy.

Familiarize yourself with this section, as well as the section "The Game of Volleyball," for an orientation and an understanding of how to set up your practice sessions around the steps.

Follow the same sequence each step (chapter) of the way:

1. Read the explanations of what is covered in this step, why the step is important, and how to execute or perform the step's focus, which may be a basic skill, concept, tactic, or combination of them.

2. Follow the numbered illustrations showing exactly how to position your body to execute each basic skill successfully. There are three general parts to each skill description: preparation phase (getting into a starting position), execution phase (performing the skill that is the focus of the step), and follow-through phase (recovering to the starting position).

3. Look over the common errors that may occur and the recommendations of how to correct them.

4. The drills help you improve your skills through repetition and purposeful practice. Read the directions and the Success Goal for each drill. Practice accordingly. Most drills require players in different positions; be sure to switch positions to practice all aspects of each drill. Record your score. Compare your score with the Success Goal for the drill. You need to meet the Success Goal of each drill before moving on to practice the next one because the drills are arranged in an easy-to-difficult progression. This sequence is designed specifically to help you achieve continued success. Pace yourself by adjusting the drills to either increase or decrease difficulty, depending on where you are.

5. As soon as you can reach all the Success Goals for one step, you are ready for a qualified observer—such as your teacher, coach, or trained partner—to evaluate your basic skill technique against the Keys to Success found at the beginning of most steps. This is a qualitative, or subjective, evaluation of your basic technique or form.

6. Repeat these procedures for each of the 12 Steps to Success. Then rate yourself according to the directions for "Rating Your Game Success."

Good luck on your step-by-step journey to enhancing your volleyball skills, building confidence, experiencing success, and having fun!

KEY

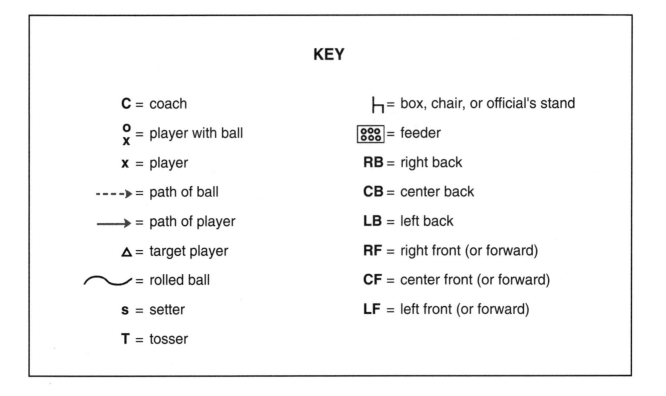

C = coach

o / x = player with ball

x = player

----▶ = path of ball

⟶ = path of player

△ = target player

∿ = rolled ball

s = setter

T = tosser

⊢ = box, chair, or official's stand

⊞ = feeder

RB = right back

CB = center back

LB = left back

RF = right front (or forward)

CF = center front (or forward)

LF = left front (or forward)

THE GAME OF VOLLEYBALL

In 1895 William G. Morgan, a YMCA director in Holyoke, Massachusetts, invented a game called *mintonette* in an attempt to meet the needs of local businessmen who found the game of basketball to be too strenuous. The new game caught on quickly because it required only a few basic skills, easily mastered in limited practice time by players of varying fitness levels. The original game was played with a rubber bladder from a basketball. Early rules allowed any number of players on a side. In 1896 the name was changed by Alfred T. Halstead, who, after viewing the game, felt that *volley ball* would be a more suitable name due to the volleying characteristic of play.

As the game has progressed, many changes in play have occurred. For example, the Filipinos are credited with adding the spike.

The game is now recognized as a strenuous sport as well as a recreational activity. The Japanese added the sport to the Olympic Games program in 1964; this contributed to the fast growth of volleyball in the last 30 years. It is currently played in 210 federations around the world. Volleyball is an exciting game for the following reasons:

- It is adaptable to various conditions that may present themselves.
- It can be played with any number on a side from two, which is extremely popular in the beach game, to six, which is the number used for interscholastic, intercollegiate, junior, and club play.
- It can be played and enjoyed by all ages and ability levels.
- It can be played on many surfaces—grass, wood, sand, and various artificial surfaces.
- It is an excellent co-ed activity.
- It is an exciting spectator sport.
- It can be played indoors or outdoors.
- It is an extremely popular recreational activity with numerous leagues in business, community, and school intramural programs.
- It requires few basic rules and skills.
- It has limited equipment needs.

Interestingly, although the game was invented in the United States, it was not until the mid-1980s that the Americans began to provide strong leadership for its development. In 1984, for the first time ever, the United States men's and women's teams won Olympic medals. The United States' men defeated Brazil to capture the gold, and the United States' women lost to China in the finals to capture the silver. The success of these two teams increased the interest level of both spectators and participants throughout the United States. In 1988, the U.S. men won the gold medal at the Seoul Olympics, and in 1992, both the men's and women's teams won bronze medals in the Olympics at Barcelona. The International Olympic Committee has added beach volleyball to the 1996 Olympics in Atlanta in response to the extremely popular beach game on the professional level. Beach volleyball players have the opportunity to win substantial purses on the professional tours.

With the impetus of the 1984 Olympic success of our American national teams, volleyball continues to grow and develop in the United States at all levels of play. The financial success of the game depends upon improving the sport's image on the spectator level. This will happen when volleyball is more visible through the media, including newspapers, magazines, and television.

Under the current scoring system in volleyball, the length of a match can vary from 1 hour to more than 3 hours, depending on how close the participating teams are in ability. This variance in time causes great consternation for the media, particularly television. Various studies have been done on different systems of scoring and time regulations that would make the game more predictable in length. Due to this problem, matches on television are not often seen in their entirety. The closely contested NCAA 1993 women's championship match between Long Beach State and Penn State, held at the University of Wisconsin, Madison, was played in front of a sold-out crowd. Only a portion of the match was shown, tape-delayed, on national television.

Beginning in the fall of 1995, the new NCAA television contract includes the live telecast of the NCAA collegiate championships for both women and men. In addition, the number of collegiate contests telecast throughout the year continues to increase. This additional coverage of collegiate volleyball will increase the spectator interest in the sport.

Playing a Game

Volleyball is played by two teams each having two to six players on a 9-meter square (about 30-feet square) court, the two courts separated by a net. The primary objective of each team is to hit the ball to the opponent's side in a manner that prevents the opponent from returning the ball. This is usually accomplished by using a three-hit combination of a forearm pass to a setter, followed by a set to an attacker, and a spike into the opponent's court.

When there are six players on a side, three are called *front row players*, and three are called *back row players*. The three players in the front row are called *left front* (LF), *center front* (CF), and *right front* (RF). (Front players are also called "Forward" players. Don't be confused—for example, the left front position and the left forward position are the *same* position.) The three players in the back row are called *left back* (LB), *center back* (CB), and *right back* (RB). Players need to be in their correct *rotational positions* until the serve is executed. This means that players cannot overlap positions from front to back or from side to side (see Diagram 1). After the serve, players are allowed to play in any position on or off the court, with one restriction: Back row players cannot leave the floor to hit the ball over the net from a position higher than the top of the net when in front of the attack line. A *side out* occurs when a team that is not serving wins the rally. When a team earns a side out, they rotate clockwise one position (see Diagram 2).

All this requires that each player master the intricacies of every one of the positions. This aspect of volleyball differentiates it from other team sports. As volleyball becomes more competitive, players are finding it increasingly difficult to learn the in-depth characteristics of all six positions. Therefore, the *specialization* of players is commonly found. When players specialize, they switch to a specific area of the court (left, center, or right) after every serve. These positions are referred to as their *playing positions*.

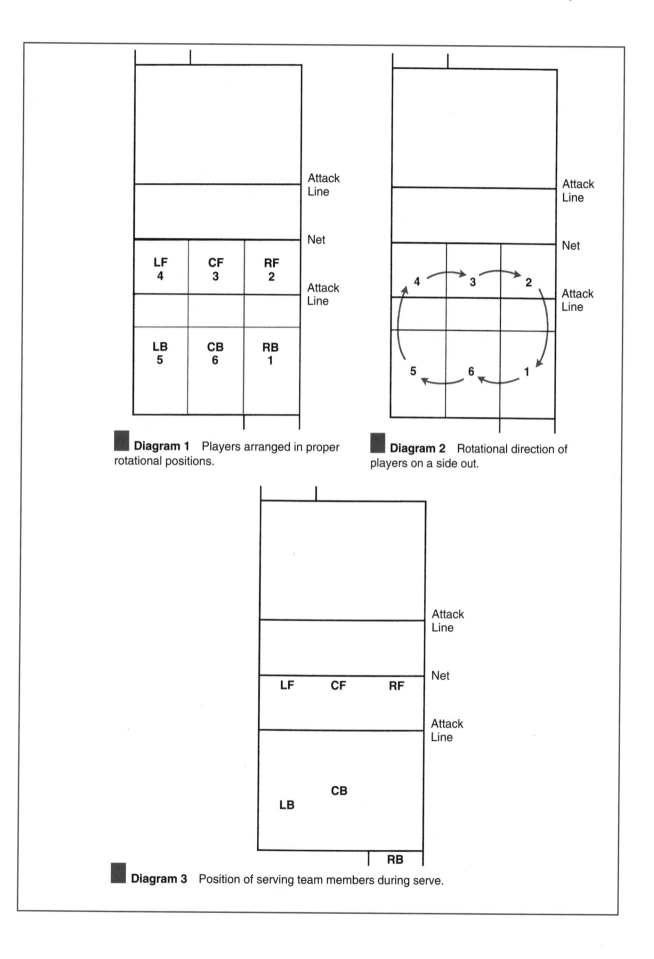

Diagram 1 Players arranged in proper rotational positions.

Diagram 2 Rotational direction of players on a side out.

Diagram 3 Position of serving team members during serve.

The serve is initiated by the right back player from a position behind the end line (see Diagram 3). In the first four games of a match, a team scores points only while it is serving, and the same player continues to serve as long as the serving team wins each rally. A *rally* is the continuous play of the ball over the net between opponents, ending in a point or side out. A point is awarded each time a team serves the ball and wins the rally. In the fifth and deciding game of the match, a point is awarded for every serve. If the serving team wins the rally, it scores a point and serves again. If the receiving team wins the rally, it scores a point and also wins the right to serve. This scoring system is referred to as *rally scoring.* A game consists of at least 15 points, and a team must be 2 points ahead to win. A match in volleyball consists of best two out of three or three out of five games. When rally scoring is used in the deciding game, the game lasts an average of 8 minutes.

Rules

Volleyball in the United States is currently being played under three sets of rules. Basically, most high schools play under the rules of the National Federation of State High School Associations; college women play under the rules of the National Association of Girls and Women in Sport (NAGWS); college men, all recreational teams, and club teams play under the United States of America Volleyball (USAV) rules. International rules govern all competition between nations. In recent years, all four sets of rules have approached uniformity. The USAV and NAGWS are identical except for substitution rules. Discussion in this book is based upon NAGWS rules.

All players should be familiar with the court markings. The volleyball court is 59 feet (18 meters) long and 29 feet 6 inches (9 meters) wide, marked by sidelines and end lines, respectively. The sidelines and end lines are part of the playing surface. Other important lines on a court are the following:

- The *centerline* divides the court into two equal playing areas, sometimes known as *team areas.*
- The *attack line* is parallel to, and 9 feet 10 inches (3 meters) from, the centerline.
- The *serving area* is the right one third of the court outside the end line, with a minimum depth of 6 feet. If this required space does not exist, a player, on the service, is allowed to step into the court up to the distance needed to make up the difference (see Diagram 4).

The correct height of the net for women is 7 feet 4-1/8 inches (2.24 meters); for men and co-ed play, 7 feet 11-5/8 inches (2.43 meters). The legal portion of the net is the part between the sidelines of the court.

A match begins with a coin toss between the teams' captains. The captain who wins the toss may choose first service, first reception, or select the team's playing area. The other captain selects from the remaining choices. The first serve rights alternate with each game until the deciding game of the match, when a second toss is made. Teams change sides at eight points in the deciding game. However, if both captains agree not to change (at the coin toss prior to that game), they may continue on the same side.

A team consists of 6 players on the court at all times. A squad cannot exceed 12 players. The lineup at the beginning of the game determines the service order throughout the game. Players of both teams must be in their correct rotational order at the time of the service by either team. The correct position of each player is described as follows:

- In the front line, the center forward must be between the right forward and the left

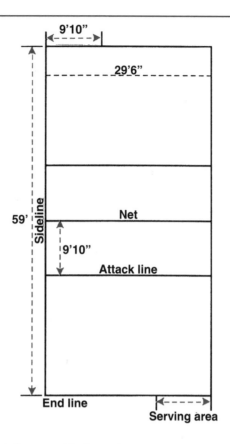

9'10"

29'6"

59'

Sideline

Net

9'10"

Attack line

End line

Serving area

Diagram 4 Basic court diagram with dimensions.

forward, and in front of the center back.

■ In the back line, the center back must be between the right back and the left back, and behind the center forward.

■ The right forward must be in front of the right back, and the left forward must be in front of the left back.

When a player is out of position, play is stopped, the error is corrected, points scored while the team was in error are canceled, and a point or a side out is awarded to the opponent.

The player in the right back position has 5 seconds to initiate the serve from the service area. The server must use one hand—either open or closed—or the arm to make contact. The ball may not touch the net and must be over the legal portion of the net. If a bad toss is made, the server may let the ball drop to the floor without touching it and begin again, being allowed an additional 5 seconds for a second attempt. The server may not step on or over the end line until after the ball is contacted.

The following rules govern contacting the ball during play:

■ Each team is allowed a maximum of three successive contacts to return the ball to the opponent's area. If the first touch is on a block, the team may have three additional contacts to return the ball. In effect, the touch on the block does not count.

■ The ball may contact any part of the body above and including the knee (USA Volleyball and International rules will allow contact by any body part beginning in 1996).

- The ball may contact any number of body parts as long as it does so simultaneously.
- When the ball comes to rest momentarily in the hand or arms of a player, it is considered *held.*
- *Double contact* is when a player hits the ball more than once with no other player touching it between these contacts. However, a player who blocks the ball may touch it a second time without an intervening touch by another player.
- If the ball is held simultaneously by two opposing players, it is a *double fault* and results in a playover.
- If two players on the same team contact the ball simultaneously (both must physically touch the ball), this is considered as two contacts for their team.
- When two opponents commit a fault simultaneously, a playover must occur.
- A player who places any part of the body above the height of the net is considered to have the intention to block; only front line players may block.
- If two players contact the ball on the block, it is considered only one hit.
- Blockers may reach over the net to block the ball as long as the opponents have hit the ball in such a manner that the ball would clearly cross the net if not touched by a defending player.

Several rules govern play near the net and at the centerline:

- The ball remains in play if it touches the legal portion of the net in play, except on the serve.
- A player may not touch the net while the ball is in play (incidental touches of the net are being allowed in USA Volleyball, International, and NAGWS rules beginning in the fall of 1995).
- If the ball is driven into the net with such force that it contacts an opponent, this is not a net fault.
- The hands may legally pass over the net after a spike on the follow-through.
- The only parts of the body allowed to touch the opponent's court are a foot or the feet; however, some part of the foot or feet must remain on or above the centerline at the time of contact.
- You can cross the *vertical plane* (an imaginary continuation of the net above and below its actual limits) as long as you don't interfere with the opponent.
- Once the ball is *dead,* it is not a fault to hit the net or cross over the centerline. A ball is dead when it has touched the playing surface, when it is ruled out-of-bounds, or when a rally has ended due to an official's whistle.
- A player may not spike the ball until part of the ball is on that player's side of the net.

Only forwards are permitted to spike or to return the ball with their hands in a position higher than the top of the net from in front of the attack line. Back line players may not block and may spike only when they take off (jump) from behind the attack line.

The ball must pass from one side of the net to the other over the legal portion of the net. A ball landing on a boundary line is considered to be in the court. A player may go off the court to play a ball. A ball coming from the opponent that is perceived to be out-of-bounds may not be caught until it legally touches an out-of-bounds area.

In NAGWS rules, 12 substitutions are allowed per game; each player may enter the game three times with the starting entry counting as one. Any number of players may enter one position in the lineup, but once a player has entered a position, they may not enter another position in that game except when injury causes the need for an unusual sub. International rules are much stricter in substitution procedures. A team is only allowed six total substitutions per game. A player may enter a game only once with the initial entry not counting. No more than two players are allowed in each rotational position unless an unusual sub is needed due to injury.

Volleyball Governance

Three governing bodies currently provide rules for volleyball competitions in the United States. Men's and women's open and men's collegiate competitions use the United States of America Volleyball (USAV) rules. For rules information and interpretation contact the USA Volleyball office: 3595 East Fountain Blvd., Colorado Springs, CO 80910-1740.

All collegiate women's play and some scholastic girls' competitions are governed by the National Association for Girls and Women in Sport (NAGWS) rules. For rules information and interpretation contact the NAGWS office: 1900 Association Drive, Reston, VA 22091.

The majority of girls' high school play and all boys' high school play is governed by the National Federation of State High School Associations (NFSHSA). For rules information and interpretation contact the NFSHSA office: 11724 Plaza Circle, Box 20626, Kansas City, MO 64195.

The USAV controls all open play in the United States. The country is divided into regions, with each region responsible for the competitive schedule for its membership. The national office in Colorado Springs can be contacted to obtain information about your regional commissioner. All commissioners have information regarding registration, player eligibility, and tournament schedules. All regions now sponsor competition for junior players.

Collegiate competition for both men and women is controlled by the National Collegiate Athletic Association (NCAA), the National Association for Intercollegiate Athletics (NAIA), or the National Junior College Athletic Association (NJCAA). These organizations oversee seasonal play and administer both national championships. Questions concerning player eligibility, national championship format, recruiting rules, and so forth should be directed to the appropriate governing bodies:

NCAA
Nall Avenue at 63rd Street
P.O. Box 1906
Mission, KS 66201

NAIA
1221 Baltimore
Kansas City, MO 64105

NJCAA
P.O. Box 7305
Colorado Springs, CO 80933

The American Volleyball Coaches' Association (AVCA) provides opportunities for coaches at all levels to share ideas and actively promote the game of volleyball. This organization also publishes a bimonthly journal, *Coaching Volleyball*, and a monthly newsletter, *American Volleyball*. Both contain new ideas and current trends in the sport. These publications are a benefit of membership in the AVCA. For more information contact the AVCA office: 122 Second Avenue, Suite 217, San Mateo, CA 94401.

Warm-Up and Cool-Down

Prior to practicing, you need a 5- to 10-minute warm-up to increase your heart rate or to "get your blood flowing." Many activities can be used to accomplish this. Running, rope jumping, sliding, cross-steps, block or spike jumps, and skipping are some examples. Generally, it is good to start easy and gradually increase your effort.

It is also important to stretch, for 10 to 20 minutes, to increase flexibility. You should stretch the body parts needed to perform all the skills so that there is no danger of pulling muscles. The best method of increasing flexibility is to stretch a muscle and remain in the stretched position for 5 to 7 seconds. The test for sufficient stretch is that you should feel the stretch of your muscle in the holding position. The arms, back, neck, legs, and feet should all be sufficiently stretched. There are many books available on the proper ways to stretch.

When your volleyball activity has been completed, spend 5 minutes cooling down. This time is used to bring your heart rate down and stretch the muscles you used most during practice. You should choose at least one flexibility exercise similar to those that you used during the warm-up, for each body part. It is recommended that each activity be executed twice. The cool-down period is important because it helps lessen the amount of soreness that you may experience when using and stretching muscle groups in a new activity.

STEP 1

BODY POSTURE: CHOOSING THE CORRECT LEVEL

You are in a game situation, and one of your teammates is spiking. You cover the spiker, close behind and in a medium to high body posture. The spiked ball is blocked and hits you in the face before you can react to dig it. Poor body posture causes you to miss this play. A low body posture should be used in this situation, which would allow you more time to react to the ball.

When you play volleyball, your body posture can be at one of three different levels—high, medium, or low. The high position is basically used for serving, setting, blocking, and spiking. When using the high position for blocking and spiking, your body can also be in the air. The medium position is the most important because it is used 70 percent of the time—during serve reception, when executing the overhead pass, and as the starting position for the spike. The low position is used during digging, during all forms of individual defense such as the sprawl and the roll, and for covering a spiker.

Why Is Body Posture Important?

Correct body posture is extremely important for volleyball performance. By using correct posture, you can perform skills more efficiently and with less chance of injury. One common error is trying to perform an individual defensive maneuver from a high posture. If you attempt to do this, you are likely to hit the floor hard due to falling from a high level, thus increasing the chance for an injury. When jumping in the air, it is important that your body be balanced before takeoff so that it will be balanced in the air. When landing from an air movement, you should cushion the landing by bending your knees to help prevent injury.

How to Execute Body Postures

High body posture is when you're either jumping in the air or standing with your feet in an easy stride with your weight evenly distributed on the balls of your feet (see Figure 1.1a). In the medium posture, your body is in an easy stride with its weight evenly distributed on the balls of your feet, your knees are bent so that they are ahead of your feet, and your shoulders lean forward so that they are in front of your knees. Your hands and arms are above your knees and away from your body (see Figure 1.1b). In the low posture, your weight is forward, your knees are bent more than 90 degrees, and your arms and hands are above your knees and away from your body. When moving to the ball in a low body posture, you must get to the ball before you attempt to play it. If possible, you should play the ball before any part of your body, other than your feet, contacts the floor (see Figure 1.1c).

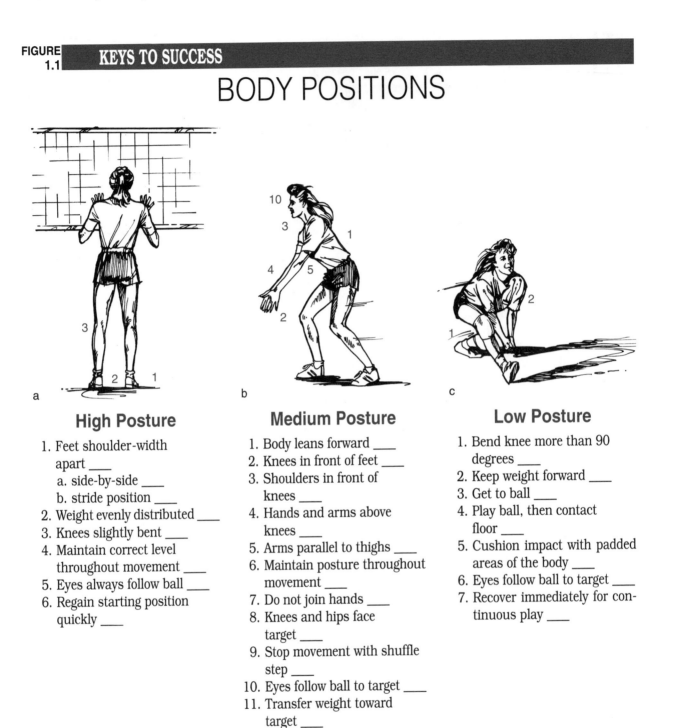

FIGURE 1.1 KEYS TO SUCCESS

BODY POSITIONS

High Posture

1. Feet shoulder-width apart ___
   a. side-by-side ___
   b. stride position ___
2. Weight evenly distributed ___
3. Knees slightly bent ___
4. Maintain correct level throughout movement ___
5. Eyes always follow ball ___
6. Regain starting position quickly ___

Medium Posture

1. Body leans forward ___
2. Knees in front of feet ___
3. Shoulders in front of knees ___
4. Hands and arms above knees ___
5. Arms parallel to thighs ___
6. Maintain posture throughout movement ___
7. Do not join hands ___
8. Knees and hips face target ___
9. Stop movement with shuffle step ___
10. Eyes follow ball to target ___
11. Transfer weight toward target ___

Low Posture

1. Bend knee more than 90 degrees ___
2. Keep weight forward ___
3. Get to ball ___
4. Play ball, then contact floor ___
5. Cushion impact with padded areas of the body ___
6. Eyes follow ball to target ___
7. Recover immediately for continuous play ___

BODY POSTURE SUCCESS STOPPERS

Errors in posture fall into two categories: (a) selecting the incorrect posture for the skill being performed or (b) selecting the correct posture but executing it poorly. Body postures should be practiced so that they become natural movements to you. Eventually, you will automatically assume the correct body posture for the skill you anticipate.

ERROR	CORRECTION
1. Your hands are too close to your body.	1. Your hands must be far enough away from your body so that your arms are parallel to your thighs.
2. You move with your hands joined.	2. Your hands should not be joined during movement, but should be quickly joined before ball contact.
3. You slam into the floor following a defensive move.	3. Your body must be in a low position and as close to the ball as possible *before* contact.
4. On defense, you do not move through the ball.	4. You must contact the ball and continue by moving toward the target.

BODY POSTURE

DRILLS

1. Mirror Drill

This drill allows you to work on agility while in the medium posture. You move quickly with frequent changes in direction—the type of movement you use in game play.

The leader stands in front, facing you and the other players. All players are in the medium body posture. The leader moves forward, backward, left, or right. You must follow the leader. Maintain the medium body posture throughout the drill.

Success Goal = continuous movement for 60 seconds, maintaining the medium body posture ___

Success Check
• React to leader___
• Move quickly___
• Maintain posture___

To Increase Difficulty
• Increase the pace of the movement.
• Change direction frequently.
• Change the body posture frequently.
• Move for a longer period of time.

To Decrease Difficulty
• Emphasize correct movement at a slow pace.
• Change direction infrequently.
• Move for a shorter period of time.

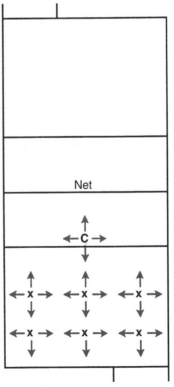

2. Forward and Backward Movement

This drill simulates movement away from the net in a medium body posture. This movement is used in a free ball situation when you are in transition from defense to offense.

Stand in the medium body posture on the attack line, facing the net. With a step, step together, move forward, touch the centerline with your foot, and move back to the attack line.

Success Goal = continuous movement with the medium body posture for 30 seconds ___

Success Check
• Step, step together forward ___
• Touch line ___
• Maintain posture ___

To Increase Difficulty
• Player touches the line with the palm of the hand.
• Lengthen the time.
• Lengthen the distance.

To Decrease Difficulty
• Player does not have to touch line.
• Continuous movement could last for a shorter period of time.
• Shorten the distance.

Net

3. Block and Roll

In this drill you practice movement in two body postures: high for the blocking action of jumping and reaching over the net, low for recovering from the floor, and high for blocking readiness.

Stand at the net in a high body posture, with your elbows bent and close to your body, and your hands in front of your shoulders. Jump, reach over the net without touching it, then quickly withdraw your hands. Return to the floor in low body posture, sit and roll onto your back, and quickly return to the starting position.

Success Goal = 10 consecutive jumps and rolls without touching the net ___

Success Check
• Jump high ___
• Reach forward ___
• Withdraw quickly ___

To Increase Difficulty
• Lower the height of the ball on the opposite side of the net.

To Decrease Difficulty
• Lower the net.

4. Low to Floor Sit

In this drill you practice moving in a low body posture to the side and hitting the floor in preparation for a roll. The lower you get to the floor, the easier the roll will be to execute.

Begin at the center of the court, facing the net in a low body posture, with your hands touching the floor. Maintaining the low posture, slide to the right sideline. At the sideline, take a big step to the side, sit on the floor, then stand and quickly return to the starting position. Repeat this movement to the left. Continue this drill, alternating right and left.

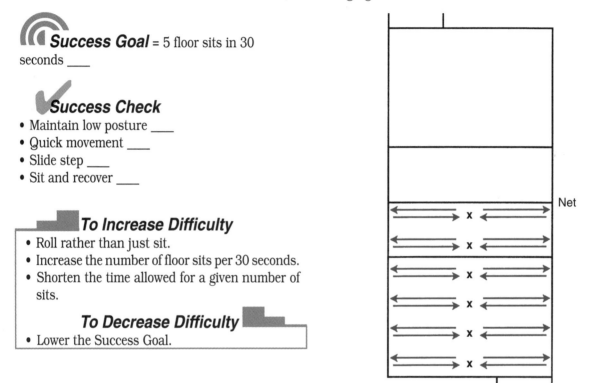

Success Goal = 5 floor sits in 30 seconds ___

✔ Success Check
• Maintain low posture ___
• Quick movement ___
• Slide step ___
• Sit and recover ___

To Increase Difficulty
• Roll rather than just sit.
• Increase the number of floor sits per 30 seconds.
• Shorten the time allowed for a given number of sits.

To Decrease Difficulty
• Lower the Success Goal.

BODY POSTURE SUCCESS SUMMARY

Often your selection of body posture is an important part of skill execution. Being in a low body posture during spike coverage allows you more time to react to a ball rebounding quickly off an opponent's block. Even though the same high body posture is used for the three different skills—serving, setting, and blocking—the starting positions of the extremities differ. For example, if you anticipate a block, your feet should be side by side, your hands at shoulder height. However, if you anticipate a set, your feet should be in a stride, with your hands above your forehead. This is true for all body postures—high, medium, and low.

Have a trained observer watch your movement patterns. The facets in the Keys to Success (Figure 1.1a-c) should be checked in the course of your performance. Such an evaluation can help you focus on actions that need extra practice.

STEP 2

FOREARM PASS: ATTACKING STARTS HERE

The game has begun. The opponent has won the toss and elected to serve first. Their first server has a powerful topspin serve that drops quickly. Six points have been scored and your team seems unable to stop the server. You can only hope that the next serve will go into the net.

Serve reception is critical to overall team success. To improve the efficiency of serve reception, the Japanese introduced and popularized the forearm pass before the 1964 Olympics. In recent years, many teams have developed players who specialize as passers during serve reception. This is done to take advantage of the special talents of these individuals as efficient forearm passers. Some teams receive with as few as two players. The United States' men's team has used only two players to receive serve since the 1984 Olympics.

The forearm pass is the first basic volleyball skill you should learn. This skill is also referred to as the *underhand pass* or the *bump*. It usually is the first skill your team must execute if you have not elected to serve. It is used to receive serves, receive spikes, play any ball at waist height or lower, and play any ball that has gone into the net. Due to the fact that this skill is used almost exclusively for receiving, it is often referred to as just a pass.

Why Is the Forearm Pass Important?

Although the forearm pass is frequently used, you have better passing control when utilizing the overhead pass (discussed in Step 4). Therefore, if possible, use the overhead pass. However, any hard-driven ball—that is, a serve or a spike—should be received with a forearm pass because open hands are not strong enough to receive a ball hit with force.

The forearm pass is most often used to direct the ball to a teammate. It is important to absorb the force of a hard-hit ball and direct the ball in such a way that your teammate can execute an overhead pass or set on the next play.

The forearm pass must be executed efficiently if your team is to be successful; it is the starting point of a successful attack. If the ball is passed poorly, the setter will have difficulty placing the ball in the best position for the attacker.

How to Execute the Forearm Pass

The basic elements for good execution of the forearm pass are (a) getting to the ball, (b) setting your position, (c) making contact, and (d) following the flight of the ball to the target. When performing the forearm pass, your hands must be joined together; your thumbs must be parallel. Your elbows are rotated inward so that the soft, flat portions of your forearms face the ceiling. This *platform* formed by your arms should be as even as possible. Your arms should be parallel to your thighs; hold them away from your body. You must try to position your body behind the ball, absorb the force, and direct the ball to the target using your body, through leg extension, while contacting the ball with little or no arm swing (poking action). See Figure 2.1 for the forearm pass Keys to Success.

The forearm pass is a relatively easy skill to perform when you move to the ball first; that is, when you get to the proper position before attempting the skill. The difficulty in the skill is that you probably do not use your forearms in performing any other sport skill. The tendency, therefore, is to hit the ball with the hands; be careful not to acquire this habit.

FIGURE 2.1

KEYS TO SUCCESS

FOREARM PASS

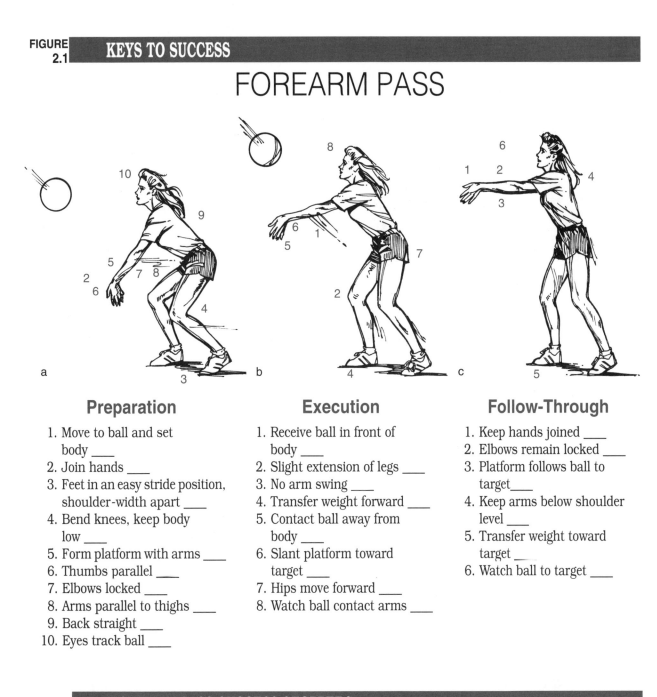

a   b   c

Preparation

1. Move to ball and set body ___
2. Join hands ___
3. Feet in an easy stride position, shoulder-width apart ___
4. Bend knees, keep body low ___
5. Form platform with arms ___
6. Thumbs parallel ___
7. Elbows locked ___
8. Arms parallel to thighs ___
9. Back straight ___
10. Eyes track ball ___

Execution

1. Receive ball in front of body ___
2. Slight extension of legs ___
3. No arm swing ___
4. Transfer weight forward ___
5. Contact ball away from body ___
6. Slant platform toward target ___
7. Hips move forward ___
8. Watch ball contact arms ___

Follow-Through

1. Keep hands joined ___
2. Elbows remain locked ___
3. Platform follows ball to target___
4. Keep arms below shoulder level ___
5. Transfer weight toward target ___
6. Watch ball to target ___

FOREARM PASS SUCCESS STOPPERS

If you learn to recognize the components of correct execution of the forearm pass, it becomes easier for you to analyze your attempts and your fellow play-ers' attempts to perform correctly. The most com-mon forearm pass errors are listed here, along with suggestions on how to correct them.

ERROR	CORRECTION
1. Your arms are too high when you contact the ball. Your arms follow through above shoulder height.	1. Let the ball drop to waist level before contact. Try to stop your arms on contact by using a "poking" action on the ball.

ERROR	CORRECTION
2. You get low by bending at your waist instead of your knees, causing you to pass the ball too low and too fast.	2. Bend your knees, keeping your back straight as you move under the ball; touch the floor with your hands to stay in a low position.
3. You do not transfer weight toward the intended target; as a result, the ball does not travel forward.	3. Check that your weight ends up on your forward foot and that your body is inclined forward.
4. Your hands separate before, at, or just after contacting the ball, resulting in an errant pass.	4. Keep your hands joined by interlocking your fingers or wrapping one hand in the other with thumbs parallel.
5. The ball contacts your arms at or above your elbows or contacts your torso.	5. Keep your arms parallel to your thighs and contact the ball away from your torso.

FOREARM PASS

DRILLS

1. Passing a Held Ball

This drill helps you to practice contacting the ball at a low level and projecting it forward. Because the ball is stationary, you can work on ball contact and body position without worrying about moving to the ball. It will be difficult to project the ball over your partner's head if you do not contact it with the arms away from the body.

Have a partner loosely hold the ball out toward you at waist level. Using forearm pass technique, hit the ball out of your partner's hands so that it is directed back over your partner's head. Your partner then retrieves the ball, and the drill continues.

Success Goal = 25 good forearm passes in 30 attempts ___

Success Check
• Ball held low___
• Weight transferred forward___
• Arms parallel to thighs___

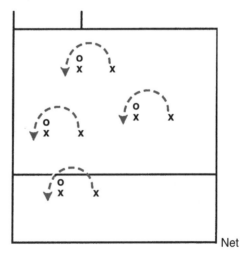

Net

2. Partner Pass

This drill allows you to pass a ball that is coming right at you. It is good to work on passing consistency from the beginning. Here you are forced to pass the ball the same distance all the time. Try also to work on consistency in the height of the pass.

Have a partner toss you a ball; using your forearms, pass the ball back to your partner. Your partner must be able to catch your pass without taking more than one step in any direction.

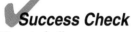 **Success Goal** = 20 good forearm passes in 25 attempts ___

Success Check
• Move to ball ___
• Set position ___
• Direct ball with platform ___

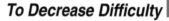 **To Increase Difficulty**
• The tosser throws the ball lower and harder, to either side of the passer or out in front of the passer.

To Decrease Difficulty
• The tosser throws the ball higher.
• Shorten the distance between partners.

3. Continuous Bumping

This drill allows you to practice consistency in your form, adds some footwork, and also assists you in letting the ball drop to you. Consistency in the height of the pass is important.

Gently toss a volleyball underhand to yourself and use forearm pass technique to keep the ball in the air. Bump the ball 8 to 10 feet high by using the net as a guide. Stay within a 10-foot square.

Success Goal = 25 consecutive bumps while remaining in the 10-foot square ___

Success Check
• Receive ball low ___
• Extend legs ___
• Control ball ___
• Aim high ___

To Increase Difficulty
• Make the playing area smaller than a 10-foot square.
• Make a quarter-turn between each contact.
• Touch the floor with a hand between each contact.

To Decrease Difficulty
• Let the ball bounce on the floor between contacts.
• Make the playing area larger than a 10-foot square.

4. Passing to Target

The tosser in this drill can control the difficulty level of the drill. The tosser can begin by tossing right at the player and, as the player becomes proficient, increase the challenge by moving the toss to the left or right.

In a group of three, one person tosses a ball over the net to you. Receive the ball and direct it using a forearm pass to a third person positioned at the net. The target catches the ball and returns it to the tosser.

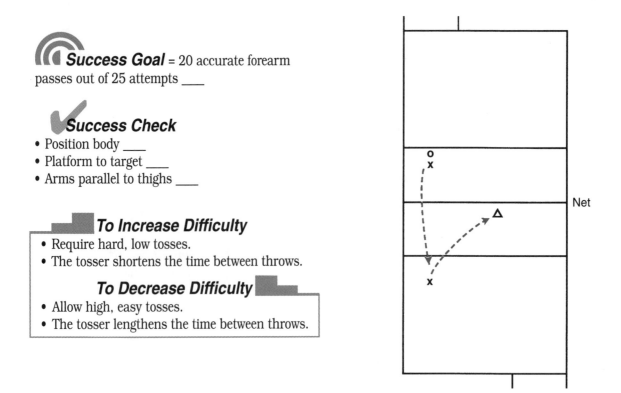

Success Goal = 20 accurate forearm passes out of 25 attempts ___

✔ **Success Check**
- Position body ___
- Platform to target ___
- Arms parallel to thighs ___

To Increase Difficulty
- Require hard, low tosses.
- The tosser shortens the time between throws.

To Decrease Difficulty
- Allow high, easy tosses.
- The tosser lengthens the time between throws.

5. Pass and Move

Practicing movement to the ball and then passing to a target is the object of this drill. Rarely in a game setting is the serve directed right at a player. This drill requires you to move into position before passing the ball.

In a group of three, have two partners stand 20 feet apart on the attack line, facing the end line. You are to face the net and move laterally (left and right) to the spots directly in front of the other two players. As you approach one of the spots, the player aligned with it tosses the ball. You receive the ball by forearm passing it back at least 2 feet higher than the height of the net. The tosser should not have to move more than one step in any direction to catch your pass.

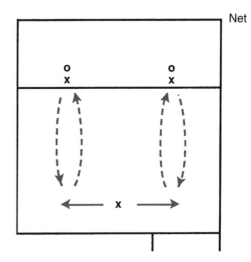

Success Goal = 20 accurate forearm passes out of 25 attempts ___

✔ **Success Check**
- Move to ball ___
- Call for ball ___
- Square to target ___
- Pass high ___

To Increase Difficulty
- The tosser throws the ball lower and sooner.
- Increase the distance between the tossers.

To Decrease Difficulty
- The tosser throws the ball higher and easier.
- The tosser waits for the passer to get into position before tossing the ball.

6. Forearm Pass for Accuracy

Once you have become proficient in the technique of passing, begin working on situations that are more gamelike. In this drill you receive a toss in the area of the court where you would most likely receive the serve, and you pass to the position on the court where your teammate would be most likely to receive it.

Have a partner stand on the attack line on the side of the court. You stand near the middle of the end line in the back third of the other side of the court.

Your partner tosses a ball to either side. Move to receive and forearm pass the ball to a 10-foot square target area on your side of the court between the attack line and the centerline. The target should begin 5 feet from the right sideline and extend 10 feet into the center of the court. Your pass should reach a height of 2 feet above the net.

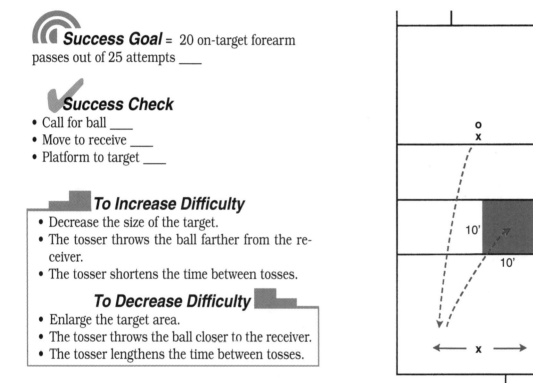

Success Goal = 20 on-target forearm passes out of 25 attempts ___

✔ **Success Check**
• Call for ball ___
• Move to receive ___
• Platform to target ___

To Increase Difficulty
• Decrease the size of the target.
• The tosser throws the ball farther from the receiver.
• The tosser shortens the time between tosses.

To Decrease Difficulty
• Enlarge the target area.
• The tosser throws the ball closer to the receiver.
• The tosser lengthens the time between tosses.

FOREARM PASS SUCCESS SUMMARY

During serve reception, a trained observer analyzing a bad pass should observe the action of the ball and be able to identify your performance error. For example, if the ball goes straight up from your hands rather than forward, it indicates one of two possible performance errors: (a) you have not transferred your weight forward, *or*, (b) you have contacted the ball too high. With this in mind, have a trained observer check your performance for the points listed in the Keys to Success in Figure 2.1.

STEP 3

SERVE AND SERVE RECEPTION:
CONTROLLING THE GAME

Your team is fighting hard in a long rally during the deciding fifth game of a closely fought volleyball match. Finally, after several outstanding plays, the ball is set to one of your attacking players who ends the rally with a kill. Your team celebrates. You are the next server and move into the service area. You toss the ball and serve it out-of-bounds, putting a quick end to your team's momentum by giving your opponent a point and the serve.

Your next skill to master is the serve. The serve is the only skill used to put the ball into play. In the nondeciding games of a match, you earn points only when your team is serving. It is therefore important that you serve with consistency—that is, serve the ball over the net into the opponent's court at least 90 percent of the time. The serve is the only skill in volleyball in which you have total control during the execution; you are solely responsible for the result. Mistakes in serving are unforced and usually more mental than physical.

Serve reception is more difficult if the serve is powerful. Efficient serve reception is the first step in preventing your opponents from scoring and allowing your team the opportunity to score.

The Serve

There are several types of serves in volleyball, four of which will be covered here. Each has its advantages and disadvantages. Every player should master the two basic serves—the underhand serve and the overhand floater. The first priority when serving is consistency—getting the ball over the net and into the opponent's court close to 100 percent of the time. Any player can easily serve the ball underhand. Once

you are consistent in using the underhand serve, you should practice other more effective serves.

The *overhand floater* serve is the next serve to learn. The name *floater* is derived from the fact that the ball moves from side to side or up and down as it travels across the net. This happens because the ball is hit without spin. Spin stabilizes a ball in flight; without spin, the ball appears to move and jump. This movement is very similar to the "knuckling" action of a pitched baseball.

Once the two basic serves are mastered, you can begin practicing more advanced serves. Popular advanced serves include the topspin serve, the roundhouse floater serve, and the jump serve.

When performing the *topspin serve*, you hit the ball hard, imparting forward spin that causes the ball to drop quickly into the opponent's court after it crosses the net. This serve, unlike the floater serve, travels a true course once it is directed because spin stabilizes the ball.

The next serve for you to master is the *roundhouse floater serve*. Players often find it easy to get this serve over the net because it utilizes the larger muscle groups of the body. Even so, the technique is not typical of other overhand sport movements, such as throwing, and this adds to the complexity of the learning process. The ball floats and knuckles the same way as the overhand floater serve. The roundhouse floater is used extensively by the Japanese.

The most advanced serve popular today is the *jump serve*. This serve is very complex to perform, and because of this, players using it serve at a lower level of consistency. In the 1988 Olympics, the United States men won the gold medal by defeating Brazil in the finals after losing to them in a preliminary match. The difference in the two matches was the level of consistency of the Brazilians in executing the jump serve. In the first match, Brazil served at a high level of consistency and won. In the final, Brazil's consistency dropped considerably, and they lost. Instruction on how to perform the jump serve is beyond the scope of this book.

Selecting a Serve: Why and When?

The serve begins the game. Your team can continue to control the play as long as you maintain the serve. The underhand serve is the easiest one to perform. This serve, although usually easy for opponents to receive, is one that you should perform with total confidence. You should master the underhand serve with 90 percent consistency before attempting other serves.

The floater serve is initiated from a higher point than the underhand serve. The straighter trajectory that results makes the ball more difficult to receive because it comes with greater force and takes less time to travel the same distance. These two factors, along with the unpredictable floating action, make this serve effective.

The topspin serve causes the ball to travel very rapidly and drop quickly, which means that the opposing team has little time to react. This catches the opponent off guard, and the serve may be an ace (a serve that either is not touched by the receiving team or is touched by a player in a manner that prevents any further play on the ball). It is also difficult for defenders to judge whether a topspin serve will land in or out when it approaches the end line. Serves that appear to be out often drop quickly at the last second and land within the court boundaries.

The roundhouse floater serve can often be executed even if you have difficulty performing the overhand serve; because you use larger muscle groups in this serve, you do not need as much strength. You may thus find initial success with this serve before you are able to execute the overhand serve. A negative aspect of the roundhouse floater is that you do not have your eyes on the target area of the opponent's court before initiating the toss.

You will gain an advantage over your opponent if you are capable of executing more than one type of

Serve Summary Chart			
Serve	**Advantages**	**Disadvantages**	**When to Use**
Underhand	• Easy to execute	• Easy to receive • High trajectory	• First serve to learn • Use until you have consistency with other serves
Overhand Floater	• Ball moves in flight • Difficult to receive • Straighter trajectory	• Not as much force • Sometimes ball will rise and go out	• After consistency has been gained
Topspin	• Ball travels rapidly and drops quickly	• Ball flight is stable • More difficult to execute • Less consistency	• Mix with other serves to disrupt receivers' timing • When opponents are receiving from a deep court position • When you have a lead or have the game in control
Roundhouse Floater	• Uses larger muscle groups; less strength is needed • Can serve ball from a deeper position on the court	• Body position is not facing the target area • Form not typical of other overhand sport movements	• When there is sufficient space in the serving area

serve with consistency. The timing of each serve is so different that the players of the receiving team are constantly wondering what to expect. If each server on a team masters a different type of serve, the team may gain a strategic edge by keeping the opponent off-balance.

How to Execute the Underhand Serve

The starting position for performing the underhand serve is standing in a stride position with the leg forward on the side opposite your hitting hand and shoulders square to the net. Hold the ball about waist level, slightly to the center from your front foot, with your weight evenly distributed on both feet. Your hitting hand swings backward above waist level and then forward to contact the ball. As you swing your hand, shift your weight from the rear foot to the front foot. Just prior to contact, your holding hand drops away from the ball. Your hitting hand swings forward and up toward the top of the net. You contact the ball with an open hand, the heel of your hand cutting into the back of the ball just below its center. Watch the flight of your serve and prepare for further action (see Figure 3.1). In beach volleyball, this serve is often used with a very high trajectory causing your opponents to look into the sun and lose the ability to track the ball.

FIGURE 3.1 **KEYS TO SUCCESS**

UNDERHAND SERVE

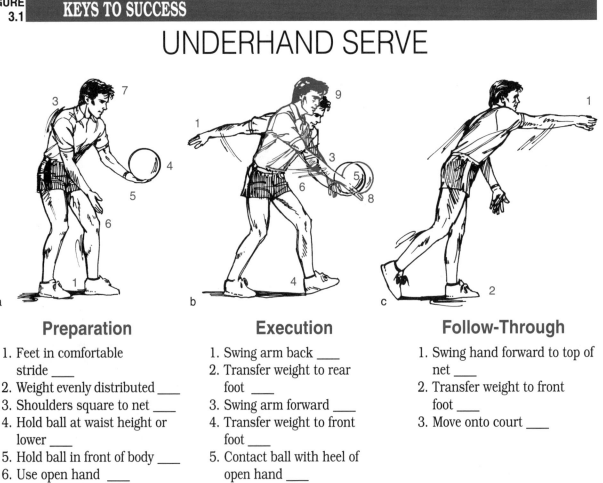

a **b** **c**

Preparation

1. Feet in comfortable stride ___
2. Weight evenly distributed ___
3. Shoulders square to net ___
4. Hold ball at waist height or lower ___
5. Hold ball in front of body ___
6. Use open hand ___
7. Eyes on ball ___

Execution

1. Swing arm back ___
2. Transfer weight to rear foot ___
3. Swing arm forward ___
4. Transfer weight to front foot ___
5. Contact ball with heel of open hand ___
6. Contact ball at waist level ___
7. Drop holding hand ___
8. Contact ball below center back ___
9. Concentrate on ball ___

Follow-Through

1. Swing hand forward to top of net ___
2. Transfer weight to front foot ___
3. Move onto court ___

How to Execute the Overhand Floater Serve

The essential element in executing the floater serve is the toss. The toss must be just in front of your hitting shoulder at a height that allows you time to swing your arm and still contact the ball at full extension. The toss must be made with little or no spin on the ball. Stand with a slight stride position, shoulders square to the net, foot of your noncontact side forward, and your weight evenly distributed. As you toss the ball, bring your hitting arm back with the elbow high and hand close to your ear. As you swing your arm forward toward the ball, keep your eyes on the ball. Make contact with the heel of your open hand slightly below the center back of the ball. The ball contact is a poking action with little or no follow-through. As your arm swings through the ball, your weight is transferred to your front foot. Continue forward to assume a defensive position. The key to consistent serving is the elimination of all extraneous movements, for example, extra steps and unnecessary or tennislike follow-through (see Figure 3.2).

FIGURE 3.2

KEYS TO SUCCESS

OVERHAND FLOATER

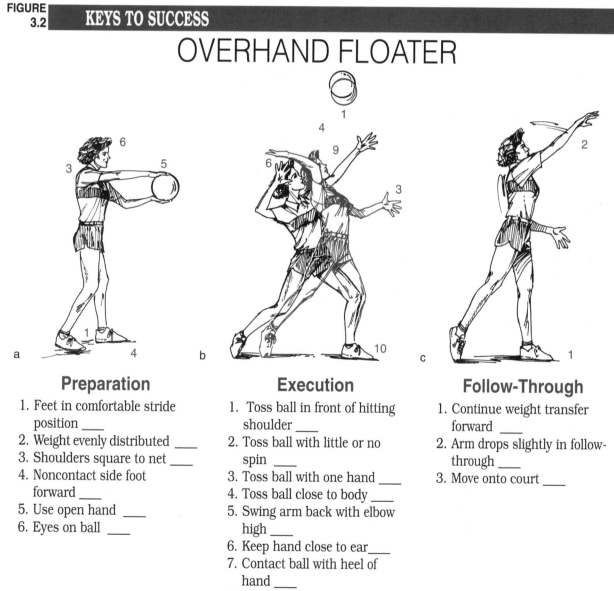

Preparation

1. Feet in comfortable stride position ___
2. Weight evenly distributed ___
3. Shoulders square to net ___
4. Noncontact side foot forward ___
5. Use open hand ___
6. Eyes on ball ___

Execution

1. Toss ball in front of hitting shoulder ___
2. Toss ball with little or no spin ___
3. Toss ball with one hand ___
4. Toss ball close to body ___
5. Swing arm back with elbow high ___
6. Keep hand close to ear ___
7. Contact ball with heel of hand ___
8. Keep arm extended at contact ___
9. Track ball to contact ___
10. Transfer weight forward ___

Follow-Through

1. Continue weight transfer forward ___
2. Arm drops slightly in follow-through ___
3. Move onto court ___

How to Execute the Topspin Serve

The topspin serve is similar in execution to the other serves. In the beginning position, turn your shoulders slightly to the sideline. Point your forward foot toward a net post. Place the ball toss slightly behind your hitting shoulder. Contact the ball just below its center back with your arm at full extension; immediately follow with a wrist snap, causing the fingers to roll over the top of the ball. The hitting hand forcibly drops down to the waist (see Figure 3.3).

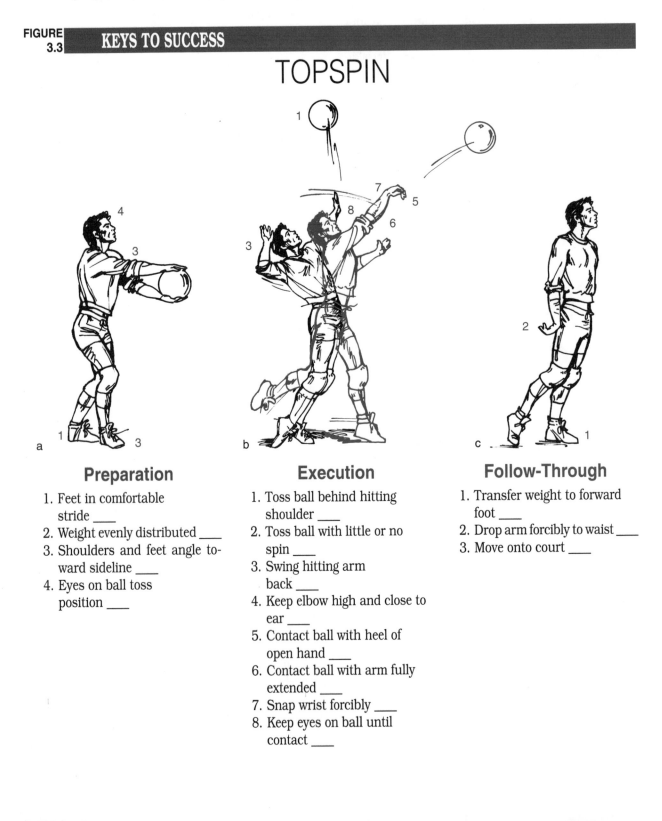

FIGURE 3.3

KEYS TO SUCCESS

TOPSPIN

Preparation

1. Feet in comfortable stride ___
2. Weight evenly distributed ___
3. Shoulders and feet angle toward sideline ___
4. Eyes on ball toss position ___

Execution

1. Toss ball behind hitting shoulder ___
2. Toss ball with little or no spin ___
3. Swing hitting arm back ___
4. Keep elbow high and close to ear ___
5. Contact ball with heel of open hand ___
6. Contact ball with arm fully extended ___
7. Snap wrist forcibly ___
8. Keep eyes on ball until contact ___

Follow-Through

1. Transfer weight to forward foot ___
2. Drop arm forcibly to waist ___
3. Move onto court ___

How to Execute the Roundhouse Floater Serve

Stand facing the sideline with your forward foot toward a net post. Toss the ball slightly ahead of your body, away from the midline and toward your nonhitting shoulder. Fully extend your arm throughout the entire motion of the serve. Drop your arm back and then swing it up over your head, making contact with the ball directly in front of your body. As you swing your arm, shift your weight forward onto your front foot, rotate your hips forward, and immediately follow with your shoulder bringing your hitting arm into contact with the ball. The contact is with an open hand just below the center back of the ball—a "poking" action with no wrist snap and little follow-through. Turn your body and move toward the court (see Figure 3.4).

FIGURE 3.4 **KEYS TO SUCCESS**

ROUNDHOUSE FLOATER

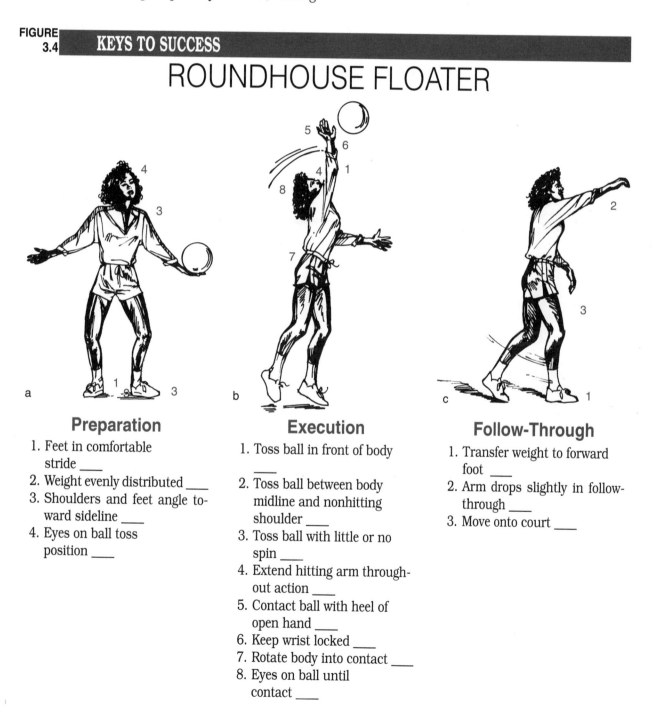

Preparation

1. Feet in comfortable stride ___
2. Weight evenly distributed ___
3. Shoulders and feet angle toward sideline ___
4. Eyes on ball toss position ___

Execution

1. Toss ball in front of body ___
2. Toss ball between body midline and nonhitting shoulder ___
3. Toss ball with little or no spin ___
4. Extend hitting arm throughout action ___
5. Contact ball with heel of open hand ___
6. Keep wrist locked ___
7. Rotate body into contact ___
8. Eyes on ball until contact ___

Follow-Through

1. Transfer weight to forward foot ___
2. Arm drops slightly in follow-through ___
3. Move onto court ___

SERVE SUCCESS STOPPERS

Underhand serve errors can usually be attributed to the position of the holding hand. Overhand floater and roundhouse serve errors usually are due to bad tosses. Good placement of the ball on the toss is essential.

The topspin serve is difficult to master because proper hand contact with the ball, the amount of wrist snap, and where the ball is contacted in relation to your hitting shoulder are critical. A slight deviation from the proper technique can cause an extreme deviation in the resulting serve. You should execute the serve with exactly the same form every time, changing only the angle of your body to change the direction of the ball. The elimination of extraneous movements helps to increase serving success.

ERROR	CORRECTION
Underhand	
1. The ball goes up, more than forward, and does not travel over the net.	1. Hold the ball at waist level or lower. Contact the ball just below center back and swing arm forward toward the net. Transfer your weight to your forward foot.
2. The ball does not have enough force to make it over the net.	2. Do not swing holding hand; hit a stationary ball. Contact must be made with the heel of your open hand.
3. Your weight ends up on your back foot; the ball trajectory is too high.	3. Step forward onto your front foot as you contact the ball. Your head and shoulders should end up forward of your knees.
Overhand Floater	
1. The ball goes into the net.	1. Be sure toss is close to the shoulder of your hitting hand.
2. The serve goes off to the right (Note: This is true for both right- and left-handed players).	2. The toss must be in front of your body, not to its right side.
3. The serve lacks the power to reach the net.	3. Use your entire body when you serve; contact the ball with the heel of your hand, not only with the fingers.
4. The ball goes over the end line of your opponent's court.	4. Make contact just below the ball's center back; make sure you contact the ball in front of your body.
5. You must take steps to reach a toss that is too far out in front.	5. Check for toss accuracy; the toss must be close to your body, just in front of your hitting shoulder.
Topspin	
1. The ball goes into the net.	1. Toss the ball behind the shoulder of your hitting hand.
2. The ball goes to the right.	2. The toss must be in front of your body, not outside your hitting shoulder.

ERROR	CORRECTION
3. The serve does not reach the net.	3. Transfer your weight at contact. Contact the ball with the heel of an open hand.
4. The ball goes over the end line of the opponent's court.	4. Contact the ball below center back, and snap your wrist forcibly, rolling your fingers over the top of the ball; finish by dropping the hitting hand to your waist.
5. You take two or three steps to serve the ball.	5. Toss the ball slightly behind your shoulder and transfer your weight forward.
Roundhouse Floater	
1. The ball goes into the net.	1. The toss is too far ahead of your nonhitting shoulder or too low.
2. The serve does not reach the net.	2. Rotate your body into the contact; contact the ball with the heel of an open hand.
3. The ball goes over the end line of the opponent's court.	3. Contact the ball to the nonhitting side of your body, just below the center back of the ball.
4. You take two or three steps to serve the ball.	4. The toss must be between the midline of your body and your nonhitting shoulder as well as close to your body. Steps are extraneous.

Receiving the Serve

By this point, you have learned movement patterns in volleyball and the skills of forearm passing and serving. You are now ready to combine these skills as they would be used in a game situation.

Why Is Serve Reception Important?

The reception of serve is the starting point of your team's attempt to gain a side out. A successful serve reception allows your team to begin your attack and hopefully win the rally. Gaining a side out prevents your opponents from scoring and gives your team the opportunity to serve and score. Remember, in a nondeciding game, you score points only when serving. To successfully receive the serve, you must be able to anticipate the direction of the ball and to de-termine whether you are the one who is going to receive it. The sooner you determine that you will receive the serve, the more time you have to get into the correct position.

How to Receive Serve

The typical serve comes to the receiver with a good deal of force. Even though the rules do not stipulate that the serve must be received by using a forearm pass, volleyball officials tend to accept only this method of playing the serve.

The best means of predicting the direction of the opponent's serve is to concentrate on the server's body. You should look for the angle of the server's shoulders, where the forward foot is pointing, and the direction of the hitting arm. The sooner that you can determine the serve direction, the better your chance of executing a good pass. It is even possible for you to cover the entire court by yourself and touch every serve if you pay attention to the server's body cues. You must call for the ball by yelling "I have it" or "mine." This call should be made before the ball crosses the net and arrives in your court. After calling for the ball, you must quickly move to the correct location to receive the serve, set your position, and execute the pass.

SERVE AND SERVE RECEPTION

DRILLS

1. Ball Toss

This drill is to improve your ability to toss the ball consistently for the overhand floater serve. Place a 12-inch-square target on the floor directly in front of and slightly to the center from your forward foot. Stand in serving position and hold your hitting hand fully extended. Toss the ball so that it goes higher than your hitting hand and lands on the target.

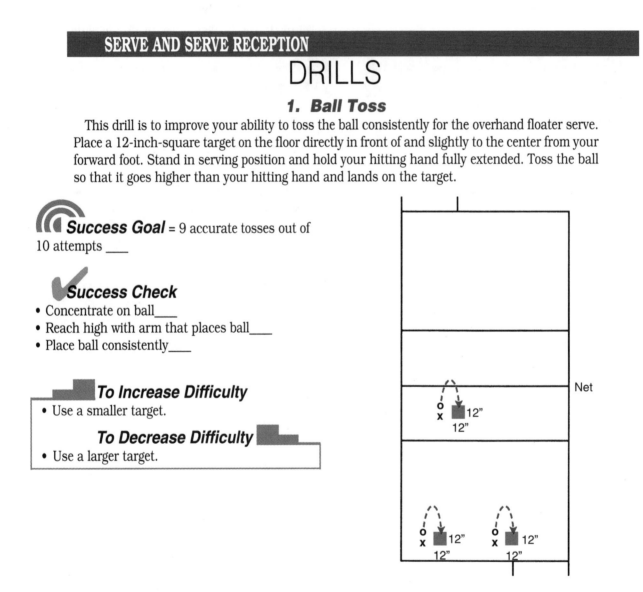

Success Goal = 9 accurate tosses out of 10 attempts ___

Success Check
• Concentrate on ball___
• Reach high with arm that places ball___
• Place ball consistently___

To Increase Difficulty
• Use a smaller target.

To Decrease Difficulty
• Use a larger target.

2. Wall Serve

This drill gives you the opportunity to work on serving form without being concerned about the distance needed to get the ball over the net.

Stand in a serving position approximately 20 feet from a wall on which is painted a line at the proper net height. Toss and serve the ball into the wall above the line.

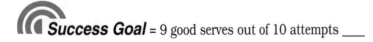 **Success Goal** = 9 good serves out of 10 attempts ___

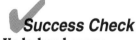
Success Check

- **Underhand serve:**
  Contact ball at waist ___
  Holding hand does not move ___
  Follow through to "top of net" (line on wall)___
- **Overhand Floater serve:**
  Shoulders square to net ___
  Place ball into position ___
  Continuous movement of serving arm after ball
    toss ___
  Hitting hand points to target___
- **Topspin/Roundhouse Floater serve:**
  Make accurate toss ___
  Contact with heel of open hand ___
  Limit follow-through on roundhouse___

To Increase Difficulty
- Choose a specific target above the wall line.
- Move farther away from the wall.

To Decrease Difficulty
- Move closer to the wall.

3. Partner Serve at the Net

This drill allows you to practice your serving form without being concerned about the force needed to get the ball the full distance required in a legal serve. You and your partner should stand in opposite sides of the court, each 20 feet from the net. Serve the ball cleanly (not touching the net) to your partner. Your partner must be able to catch the ball without moving more than one step.

Success Goal = 7 accurate serves out of
10 attempts ___

Success Check
- **Underhand serve:**
  Accuracy before all else___
- **Overhand Floater serve:**
  Consistent toss ___
  Consistent movement ___
  Eliminate excess body movements___
- **Topspin/Roundhouse Floater serve:**
  Toss ball accurately ___
  Make contact at full arm extension ___
  Shoulders square to partner at contact___

To Increase Difficulty
- Increase the distance between you and your partner.
- The receiver stands without moving to receive the ball.

To Decrease Difficulty
- Reduce the distance between partners.
- Lower the net.

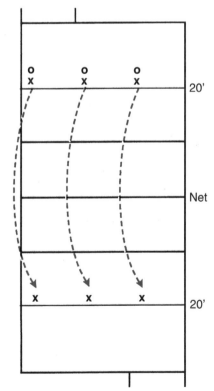

4. Simulated Serve and Forearm Pass

This drill allows you to practice accurate passing when receiving a simulated serve from a gamelike position on the court. It allows you to gain a kinesthetic awareness for the court distances. In a group of three players with two balls, the tosser is on one side of the net at the attack line (see Diagram a, below). You and the other player are on the opposite side of the net. You are the receiver, standing in the backcourt midway between the attack line and the end line. The other is a target player, standing near the net to your right.

The tosser, using a two-hand method, throws one ball over the net toward you. Call for the ball and forearm pass it higher than (not over) the net to the target, who should not have to move more than one step in any direction to catch the ball. Meanwhile, the target has delivered a second ball to the tosser. The tosser immediately tosses the second ball, then receives and tosses the first ball, and so on, making the drill continuous.

Success Goal = 20 accurate forearm passes out of 25 attempts ___

Success Check
• Anticipate well___
• Call for ball before it crosses net___
• Move, set, execute___

To Increase Difficulty
• Increase the force of the toss.
• Shorten the time between tosses.
• Tosser moves to service area and serves ball (see Diagram b, below).

To Decrease Difficulty
• Decrease the force of the toss.
• Toss directly at the receiver.
• Lengthen the time between tosses.
• The receiver may move more than one step in any direction.

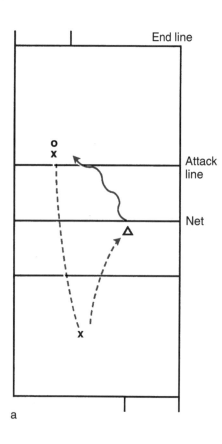

a

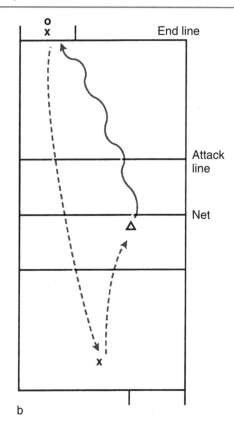

b

5. End Line Serve

This drill helps you to develop a feel for the amount of force and the angle of direction needed to serve successfully on a full court. You and your partner should stand on opposite end lines. Serve cleanly back and forth to each other's side of the court.

Success Goal =

a. 9 good underhand serves out of 10 attempts ____
   9 good overhand floater serves out of 10 attempts ____
   9 good topspin serves out of 10 attempts ____
   9 out of 10 good roundhouse floater serves out of 10 attempts ____

b. 25 consecutive underhand serves ____
   25 consecutive overhand floater serves ____
   25 consecutive topspin serves ____
   25 consecutive roundhouse floater serves ____

Success Check

• **Underhand serve:**
  Accuracy before all else ____
• **Overhand Floater serve;**
  Consistent toss ____
  Consistent movement ____
  Eliminate excess body movements ____
• **Topspin/Roundhouse Floater serve:**
  Choose direction and position body accordingly ____
  Good toss is essential ____
  Heel of hand must contact ball ____
  Follow through in direction of serve ____

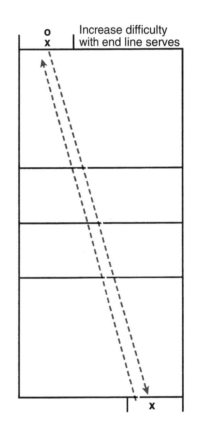

To Increase Difficulty

• Stand diagonally from partner and serve from behind the opposite end lines (see diagram).
• The server slightly changes position at the end line, creating a new angle of serve.
• Serve to only one half of the court, divided across either the width or the length.

To Decrease Difficulty

• Reduce the distance between server and the net.
• Use a lighter ball.

6. Receiving Serve From the Right/Left Back Positions

In this drill the receiver practices receiving serve from the left and right back positions on the court that correspond to the serve reception positions of traditional team formations. The passer stands either in the right or left back position, calls for the ball, and passes so that the ball is higher than the net and falls to the court in a 10-foot-square target. This target is bounded by the centerline and the attack line, and begins 5 feet from the right sideline. The target person catches the ball after it bounces, then returns it to the server. The server should serve to the half of the opposite court where the receiver is standing.

 **Success Goal** =

a. Right back position
   6 good forearm passes out of 10 attempts ___
   10 legal serves out of 12 attempts ___
b. Left back position
   6 good forearm passes out of 10 attempts ___
   10 legal serves out of 12 attempts ___

✔ **Success Check**

• Anticipate well___
• Call for ball before it crosses net___
• Move, set, execute___

To Increase Difficulty

• The server serves with a lower trajectory.
• The server serves farther away from the passer.
• Shorten the time between serves.

To Decrease Difficulty

• The server serves with a higher trajectory.
• The server serves directly at the passer.
• Lengthen the time between serves.

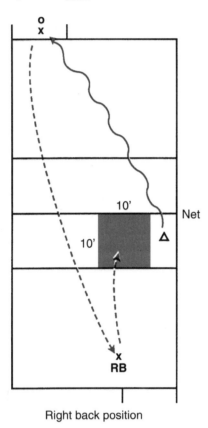

Right back position

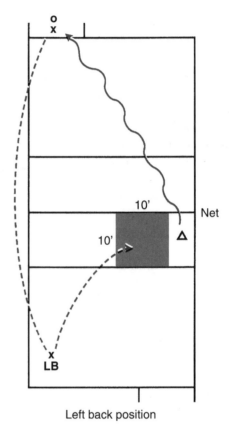

Left back position

7. Serve for Accuracy

You can gain a strategic advantage by being able to serve to your opponent's weak areas. In this drill, you practice serving accurately to all points of the court. Place a sheet approximately 10 feet square in one of the six rotational positions on one side of the court. Stand in the opposite serving area (the right third of the court) and serve, attempting to hit the target. You should attempt this drill for all six target areas.

Success Goal = 20 or fewer serves needed to hit a target 5 times, repeating for each target. Record the number of good serves needed to hit each target:

Target	Underhand	Overhand	Topspin	Roundhouse
1	_____	_____	_____	_____
2	_____	_____	_____	_____
3	_____	_____	_____	_____
4	_____	_____	_____	_____
5	_____	_____	_____	_____
6	_____	_____	_____	_____

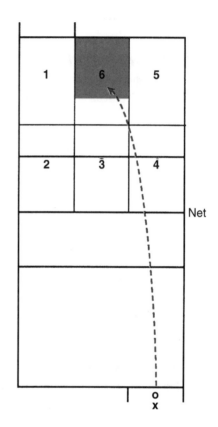

Success Check

- **Underhand/Overhand Floater serve:**
  Toe of nonhitting side foot points toward intended
    target ___
  Arm to target ___
  Transfer of weight ___
- **Topspin/Roundhouse Floater serve:**
  Accurate toss ___
  Heel of hand cuts into ball with arm at full extension ___
  Quick wrist snap when serving topspin ___

To Increase Difficulty

- Reduce the size of the target.
- Make the drill competitive: Challenge the servers on one end line to reach the Success Goal before those on the other end line.

To Decrease Difficulty

- Enlarge the target.
- Increase the number of attempts allowed for meeting the Success Goal.

8. Call and Serve

This is a competitive drill to practice serving strategically under the type of pressure similar to an actual game. In a game, the player wants to serve to an area that would give the player's team an advantage depending on the opposing players' strengths and weaknesses. Each side of the volleyball court is divided into six equal areas—three by the end line, three along the net. These areas are numbered counterclockwise, beginning with 1 in the right back position. Short (net) areas are numbered 2, 3, and 4, and long areas are 5, 6, and 1.

Indicate the area you are serving to by calling out its number prior to serving. Points are awarded as follows: 3 points for hitting the target called, 2 points if the target is missed but the serve hits an adjacent target at the same distance (both short or both long), and 1 point for a serve at the opposite distance.

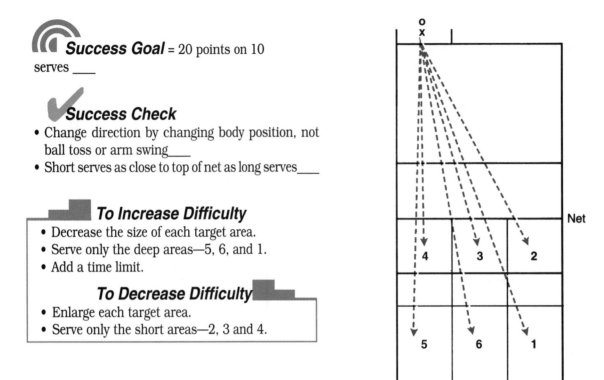

Success Goal = 20 points on 10 serves ___

✔ Success Check
- Change direction by changing body position, not ball toss or arm swing___
- Short serves as close to top of net as long serves___

To Increase Difficulty
- Decrease the size of each target area.
- Serve only the deep areas—5, 6, and 1.
- Add a time limit.

To Decrease Difficulty
- Enlarge each target area.
- Serve only the short areas—2, 3 and 4.

9. Calling the Pass

This drill allows players to become accustomed to the team concept of serve reception. It helps players to improve both in decision making and communication. In a group of four, two are receivers in the left back and right back positions, one is a target person in the right one third of the court near the net, and the fourth is a server on the opposite side of the net.

The server should vary the serves and hit them into each of the three deep positions. One or the other of the receivers should call for each serve and pass it to the target as in previous drills.

 **Success Goal =**
6 good forearm passes out of 10 attempts ___
10 serves into each of the three deep positions out of 12 attempts ___

✔ Success Check
- Call for ball___
- Move, set, execute___
- Cover for partner___

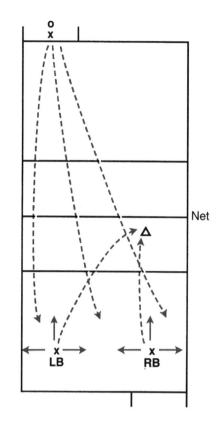

To Increase Difficulty
- The server uses a lower trajectory and more force.
- The server serves to the space between the backs (the *seam*).
- Shorten the time between serves.

To Decrease Difficulty
- The server uses a higher trajectory.
- Serve directly at the receiver.
- Lengthen the time between serves.

10. Team Serving

This drill gives you the opportunity to practice serving as a team and with the pressure of competition. The drill is more gamelike. In two teams of six each, one team groups in each service area of the court. Have plenty of volleyballs at each serving area with an equal number at each. Place 10-foot-square targets in the same rotational positions on each side of the court.

Two or three servers on each team begin serving at the target all at the same time. After serving, each player retrieves a ball and prepares to serve again. Meanwhile, other team members will step forward to serve. Servers continuously switch places after each repetition. Repeat this drill for all six target areas.

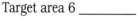 **Success Goal** = hit each of the target areas with 20 serves before your opponent for each of the six target areas:

Target area 1 _____

Target area 2 _____

Target area 3 _____

Target area 4 _____

Target area 5 _____

Target area 6 _____

Success Check
- Accurate toss___
- Arm swings to target___
- Heel of hand cuts into ball___

To Increase Difficulty
- Decrease the size of the target.
- Limit time for trying to hit each target.

To Decrease Difficulty
- Enlarge the target.
- Serve from anywhere behind the end line.

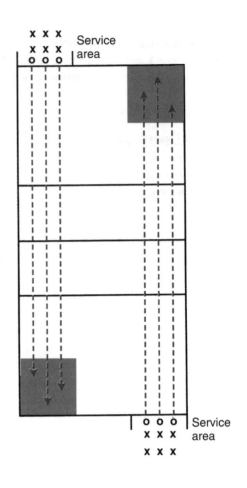

11. Minus Two

This drill also gives you the opportunity to practice serving under the pressure conditions associated with competitions. In this drill the player must serve the ball into the opponent's court or lose points, similar to losing the serve for an error in actual competition. This is almost the same as the previous drill. Here the serve needs to be only within the boundaries of the opposite court. One person serves at a time on each side. Each person serves only once followed immediately by the next person. Retrieve a ball after you've served and go to the end of the line to prepare to serve again.

For each legal serve, your team scores 1 point. For every bad serve, your team is penalized 2 points. The first team to reach 20 points wins.

**Success Goal** = 20 team points ____

Success Check
- Take your time____
- Aim____
- Use an excellent ball toss____

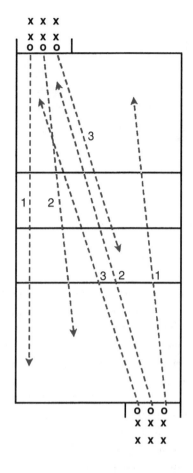

To Increase Difficulty

- Reach the Success Goal with a time limit.
- Serve to only half of the opposing court.

SERVE AND SERVE RECEPTION SUCCESS SUMMARY

Serving and receiving serve are the two most important skills in volleyball. The serve must be in the opponent's court to force the opponent to play the ball and possibly make an error. When receiving, making a good pass is critical to begin your team's offense.

Try to master the underhand serve before practicing the overhand floater serve. Practice the more advanced serves only after reaching the Success Goals for the first two. During competition use the serve that is your most efficient, but continue to practice the other serves. The more serves you can do consistently, the more effective you will be.

Ask a skilled observer to watch you perform each of the four serves. For the underhand serve, ask him or her to pay particular attention to your weight transfer (see Figure 3.1). When checking the overhand floater serve, the observer should be directly behind you to evaluate your toss (see Figure 3.2). For the topspin serve, ask the observer to watch your contact point in relation to your body (see Figure 3.3). For the roundhouse floater serve, the observer should focus on hand-ball contact (see Figure 3.4). The ball must not be spinning when it leaves your hand.

To become an efficient passer on serve reception, you should receive as many serves as possible. When practicing serve reception, receive different types of serves from different positions on the court. When evaluating serve reception, your observer should focus on your readiness to receive the serve. Your success depends on your ability to read the opposing server early, move to position, and get set to receive.

STEP 4

OVERHEAD PASS: SETTING THE ATTACK

Your team is ready to receive a free ball from the opponent. The ball is coming over the net high, easy, and directly to you. Your teammates are anticipating a strong attack in transition. Instead of using an overhead pass, you decide to allow the ball to drop and use a forearm pass. You shank the ball into the crowd; another excellent opportunity is wasted. Whenever the ball is coming to you high and easy, your choice should be the overhead pass. This is the next skill for you to learn. This skill should be the one in which you handle the ball with the greatest efficiency and the most control. You use the overhead pass to direct the ball to a teammate and, rarely, to return the ball to the opponent.

The *set* is an overhead pass that you execute to place the ball in a position for the attack. This pass is executed primarily by the setter, but it may be used by any player. The set can be either a forward pass or a back pass. The height of the set depends upon the type of spike desired. In volleyball today, the setter needs to have the capability of executing a variety of set types. A setter should be able to execute this skill either forward or backward without changing the style of delivery.

Why Is the Overhead Pass Important?

The overhead pass can be used to receive any ball higher than shoulder level and coming to the player with little force. You should use the overhead pass whenever appropriate. Do not let the ball drop to forearm pass level, because the overhead pass is the most efficient way to handle the ball.

The ultimate goal of a volleyball team on offense is to complete the three-hit sequence of pass, set, and attack. Your team must convert a hard-driven serve into a ball that is easily manageable. This requires cushioning the ball as you receive it and directing it high and easy to the setter.

The set is usually your team's second contact of the ball in the three-step offensive effort. The setter must place the ball in a position where the attacker can hit it aggressively back to the opponent. In most offensive situations, one player is designated as the setter and is the player who executes the second hit or set. The setter should be the best overhead passer on the team.

The set determines where and how well the attack develops. Setters must have outstanding ability in setting the ball. A well-placed set enhances the attacking team's ability to gain an advantage over the opponent.

Sets in volleyball are usually identified by a numbering system combining two digits. One digit indicates the height of the set above the net; the second digit indicates the spot, either on the net or in relationship to the setter, where the ball will be directed. Teams can develop play-calling systems that are quite complicated. The United States National teams are currently utilizing a three-digit system, the third digit indicating the set's distance from the net.

For the purpose of this introductory book, only three basic sets will be discussed: the high outside, the quick, and the back set. The *high outside set* is placed on the left side of the court so that, if left alone, it would drop on the left sideline. It is set at least 6 feet higher than the top of the net. In the high set, it is the attacker's responsibility to go to the ball.

The *quick set* is always set in relation to the setter. The setter sets the ball directly in front of himself or herself and 1 to 2 feet higher than the top of the net. In a quick set, it is the setter's responsibility to set the ball accurately to the attacker. The attacker approaches in front of the setter and jumps before or as the setter contacts the ball.

The *back set* needs less traveling distance than the high outside set and requires less height (5-6 feet higher than the top of the net). The back set is performed with the same technique as the front set except that as the setter contacts the ball, the back is arched and the ball is directed toward the ceiling. A good setter prepares to execute all sets exactly the same way to avoid giving the opponent any indication of the intended set (Figure 4.1).

How to Execute the Overhead Pass

The ready position is a slight stride, your feet shoulder-width apart, your knees bent, your hands raised in front of your forehead at a distance of approximately 6 to 8 inches, and your thumbs pointing toward your eyes. Form a "window" with your thumbs

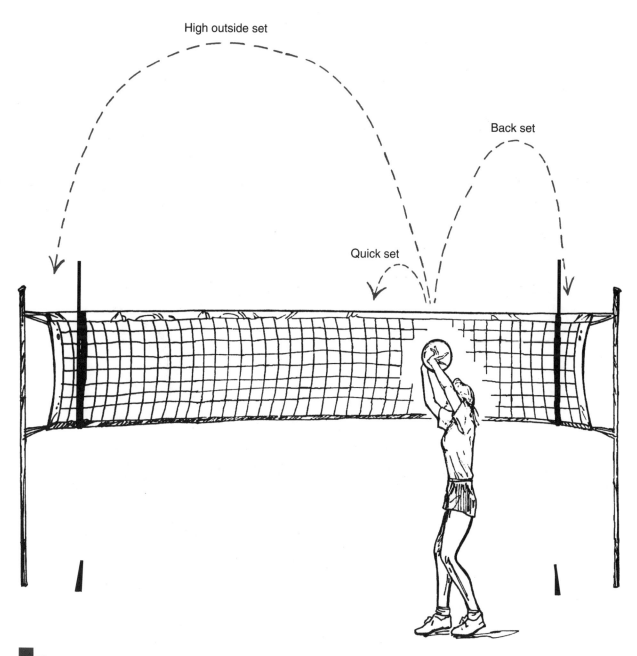

High outside set

Back set

Quick set

Figure 4.1   Ball paths for the high outside, quick, and back sets. The tape markers on the net are located directly over the sidelines

and pointer fingers in such a manner that your fingers are twice as far apart as your thumbs. Watch the ball through this window. Your shoulders should be positioned squarely toward the target. As the ball contacts your hands, your hands form to the shape of the ball with only the upper two joints of your fingers and thumbs actually touching the ball. As the ball contacts your fingers, extend your arms and legs, transferring your weight in the intended direction of the pass (see Figure 4.2).

The setter takes a position on the right side of the court, close to the net and facing the left sideline.

The set is executed in the same manner as the overhead pass. When you set the ball to an attacker, it should be 1 to 3 feet off (away from) the net so that the attacker can hit the ball hard without contacting the net. Many beginning setters try to place the ball too close to the net, which does not allow the attacker the necessary angles to direct the attack around the opposing block. If a set is not perfect, it is better that it be farther than 1 to 3 feet from the net, rather than closer to it. A ball away from the net can be successfully attacked, but one too close to the net is generally impossible to hit past the block.

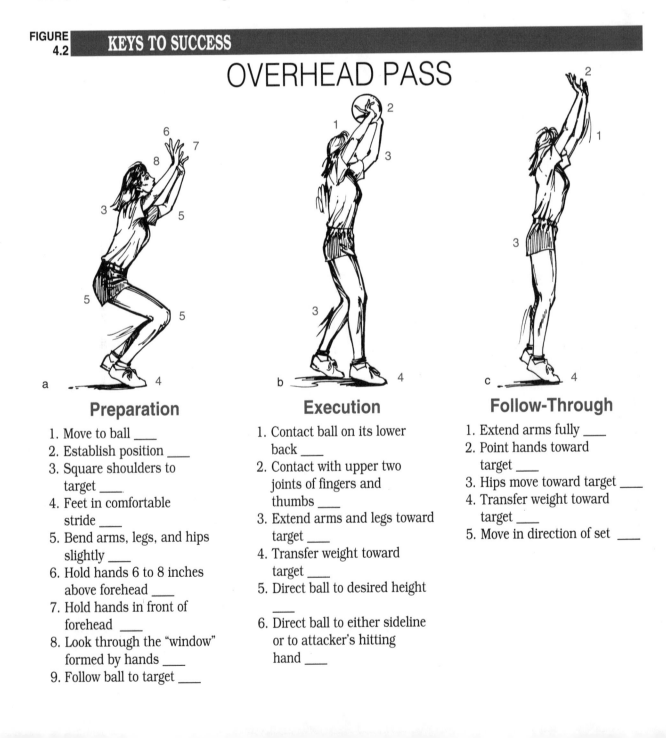

FIGURE 4.2

KEYS TO SUCCESS

OVERHEAD PASS

Preparation

1. Move to ball ___
2. Establish position ___
3. Square shoulders to target ___
4. Feet in comfortable stride ___
5. Bend arms, legs, and hips slightly ___
6. Hold hands 6 to 8 inches above forehead ___
7. Hold hands in front of forehead ___
8. Look through the "window" formed by hands ___
9. Follow ball to target ___

Execution

1. Contact ball on its lower back ___
2. Contact with upper two joints of fingers and thumbs ___
3. Extend arms and legs toward target ___
4. Transfer weight toward target ___
5. Direct ball to desired height ___
6. Direct ball to either sideline or to attacker's hitting hand ___

Follow-Through

1. Extend arms fully ___
2. Point hands toward target ___
3. Hips move toward target ___
4. Transfer weight toward target ___
5. Move in direction of set ___

OVERHEAD PASS SUCCESS STOPPERS

Players have difficulty performing the overhead pass for two major reasons: (1) they don't position themselves behind the ball with shoulders square to the target before contact, or (2) they try to play the ball with their arms and legs fully extended. It is best to move to the correct court position, then wait in a medium body posture for the ball to come down. Body position in relation to the net is also critical to good setting. If the right foot is kept forward in the stride position, the set is less likely to cross over the net. Also, this position offers full view of the net and the attacker when setting high outside.

ERROR	CORRECTION
1. The ball contacts your palms and is "held."	1. Spread your fingers, wrap them around the ball, and contact the ball with only the upper two joints of your fingers and thumbs.
2. The ball travels vertically, instead of high and toward the target.	2. Your limb extension and weight transfer should be forward toward the target. Contact the ball at its lower back, not its bottom.
3. You have difficulty directing the ball toward the target.	3. Your shoulders *must* be positioned squarely toward the target. Equal force should be imparted to the ball with each of your hands.
4. The ball spins excessively.	4. You must give the ball immediate impetus; do not roll it off your hands.
5. The set crosses the net into the opponent's court.	5. When in position at the right front of the court, you should face the left sideline and have your right foot forward.
6. The ball travels into the net.	6. When you are in position to set, your shoulders should be squarely facing the intended target.
7. The ball does not reach the sideline.	7. You must place the ball so that it will drop on the sideline. Make sure that you extend your arms and legs for additional force.
8. You set the ball too low.	8. The highest point of the set's trajectory should be 6 to 8 feet above the top of the net for the forward set, 5 to 6 feet for the back set. Extend arms upward.

OVERHEAD PASS

DRILLS

1. Pass-Bounce-Pass

This drill is particularly good for beginners who are often afraid to injure their fingers. As the ball rises from the floor, it is easier to hit because it is not gaining as much force as it would dropping from a height.

Overhead pass the ball at least 5 feet into the air, let it drop to the floor, and pass the ball again as it rises from the floor. Keep the ball in an area the size of half of one side of the court.

Success Goal = 25 consecutive overhead passes ___

Success Check
• Let ball drop ___
• Contact with upper two joints of fingers ___
• Extend arms and legs with contact ___

To Increase Difficulty
• Reduce the allowed space.

To Decrease Difficulty
• Increase the allowed space.

2. Partner Toss and Pass

In this drill you practice hitting a ball that is coming toward you and dropping from a height.

Have a partner toss a volleyball high and easy toward you. Overhead pass the ball back so that your partner can catch it without moving more than one step in any direction.

Success Goal = 8 good overhead passes to your partner ___

Success Check
• Let ball drop ___
• Contact with upper two joints of fingers ___
• Extend arms and legs with contact ___

To Increase Difficulty
• Vary the direction and height of the toss.
• Shorten the time between tosses.

To Decrease Difficulty
• Receiver allowed more steps to catch the ball.
• Lengthen the time between tosses.

3. Free Ball Passing

This drill simulates a front row player receiving a free ball in a game situation. A player who has been at the net anticipating a block hears the free ball call and moves off the net as he or she would in a game.

In a group of three players, have one be the tosser, standing on one side of the net near the attack line. You be the receiver, standing on the other side in a blocking position at the net (standing close to the net, your hands held in front of your shoulders, your fingers spread). The third player stands at the attack line as the setter.

The tosser yells "free" and then tosses the ball over the net high and to the attack line. You, the receiver, move off the net to the attack line when you hear "free." Pass the ball overhead to the setter, who has moved to the net on the "free" signal. Your passes should be 2 to 3 feet higher than the net; the setter shouldn't have to adjust the net position taken by more than one step to field your pass. The setter catches the ball and returns it to the tosser. You all return to your starting positions and practice more.

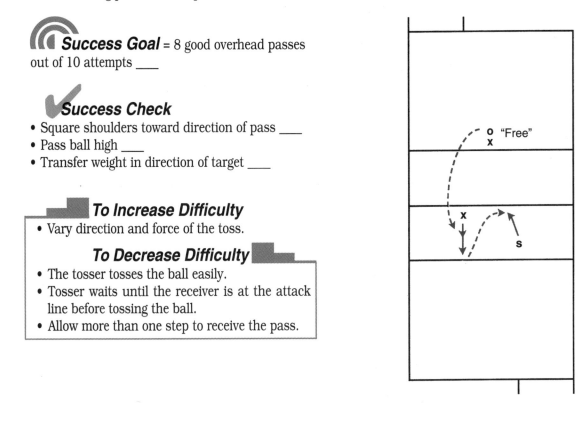

Success Goal = 8 good overhead passes out of 10 attempts ___

Success Check
• Square shoulders toward direction of pass ___
• Pass ball high ___
• Transfer weight in direction of target ___

To Increase Difficulty
• Vary direction and force of the toss.

To Decrease Difficulty
• The tosser tosses the ball easily.
• Tosser waits until the receiver is at the attack line before tossing the ball.
• Allow more than one step to receive the pass.

4. Short Pass, Back Pass, Long Pass

This drill gives players an opportunity to practice overhead passing back over their heads and overhead passing different distances.

In a group of three, stand in a line approximately 10 feet apart, two players facing in one direction and the third player facing them. The player facing the other two players initiates the drill with an overhead pass to the middle player, who back sets the ball to the third player, who then long passes the ball back to the starting player.

Success Goal = 15 consecutive three-pass sequences ___

Success Check
• Back pass action is same as overhead pass, except that back is arched at contact ___
• In back pass, ball is passed more upward than back ___
• Leg and arm extension for long pass ___

**To Increase Difficulty**
- Lengthen the distance between the players.

To Decrease Difficulty
- Shorten the distance between the players.
- Increase the height of the passes.

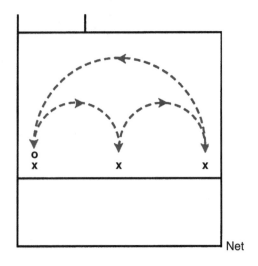

Net

5. Pass, Move, Pass

This drill allows players to work on overhead back passing footwork and ball control. It is also a good drill for conditioning.

Start this drill facing a partner. Player A overhead passes to player B and runs to a position behind player B. Player B receives the pass, overhead passes the ball to himself or herself, back passes to player A, and turns to face player A. Player A receives the pass and, keeping the ball moving, overhead passes the ball back to player B, starting the sequence over. This drill can continue indefinitely.

**Success Goal** = 10 consecutive front-back pass sequences ____

Success Check
- Pass and move quickly ____
- Higher passes allow more time ____
- Set position before passing ____

To Increase Difficulty
- Pass the ball lower.
- Player B does not pass to self before back setting.

To Decrease Difficulty
- Pass the ball higher.
- Player B sets more than once to self before back setting.

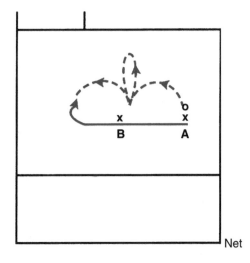

Net

6. Pass Around and Back

This drill forces players to practice passing the ball to greater heights. When practicing this drill, players soon learn that the higher they pass the ball, the easier it is to continue the drill. This is an excellent drill for conditioning.

Facing a partner as in the previous drill, player A overhead passes the ball to player B. This time, though, player A runs all the way around player B and back to the starting position. Player B, meanwhile, overhead passes the ball to himself or herself while A is circumnavigating B. When A gets back to the starting position, B overhead passes back to A. Keeping the ball moving, A starts the sequence over.

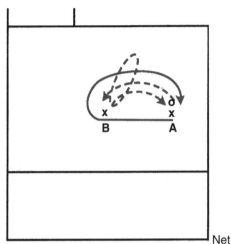

Success Goal = 10 consecutive pass-and-go sequences ___

Success Check
• Pass and move quickly ___
• Higher passes allow more time ___
• Set position before passing ___

To Increase Difficulty
• Pass the ball lower.
• Player B does not pass to self before setting to player A.

To Decrease Difficulty
• Pass the ball higher.
• Player B sets more than once to self before setting to player A.

7. High Outside Set

This drill helps you to learn the force and height needed to get the ball to the sideline of the court. Beginners often develop the tendency to set the ball too close to the net, not high enough, or not out to the sideline.

With a partner on a regulation court, stand 5 feet in from the right sideline with your partner standing just outside the left sideline.

Your partner begins the drill by tossing you the ball. You must set the ball to a height of at least 7 feet above the top of the net, and it should land within 1 foot of the left sideline.

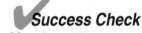

Success Goal = 15 good sets out of 20 attempts ___

Success Check
• Move to position ___
• Square to target ___
• Set forward and upward ___
• Follow to coverage ___

To Increase Difficulty
- Vary the closeness of the toss to the net.
- Increase distance between setter and target area.

To Decrease Difficulty
- Toss from directly in front of setter.

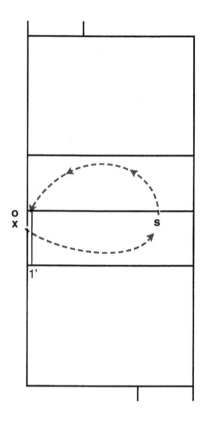

8. High Back Set

This drill allows the player to develop consistency in distance, height, and placement for a back set to the right sideline.

For this drill you need two partners. One tosses a high ball to you, the setter, as you stand 5 feet in from the right sideline, as in the previous drill. Your other partner is positioned behind you, standing just outside the right sideline. You must back set the ball to a height of at least 5 feet above the top of the net, and it must land within 1 foot of the right sideline.

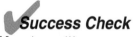**Success Goal** = 15 good sets out of 20 attempts ___

Success Check
- Move to position ___
- Square to target ___
- Set upward while arching back ___
- Turn to cover ___

To Increase Difficulty
- Vary the distance of the toss from the net.
- Vary the height of the toss.

To Decrease Difficulty
- Tosser moves closer to the setter.
- Toss from directly in front of setter.

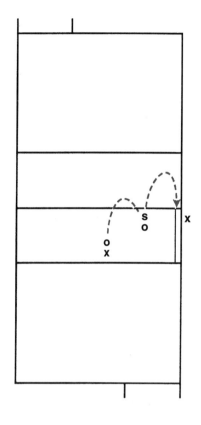

9. Quick Set

This drill helps to develop the critical timing needed between the setter and the attacker for an efficient quick attack. The attacker needs to recognize that the higher the pass to the setter, the more time the attacker has for the approach.

This drill requires one partner. The attacker begins at the attack line; the setter stands close to the net.

The attacker overhead passes the ball to the setter and quickly runs to the net. The setter quick sets the ball 1 foot in front of himself or herself and 1 to 2 feet higher than the top of the net. The attacker jumps just before or as the setter contacts the ball, raising the hitting hand as a target for the set. The attacker catches the ball, lands on both feet, and returns to the attack line. After several practice attempts switch places.

Success Goal = complete 5 sets out of 10 attempts ___

Success Check
- Setter's hand up as pass target ___
- Setter calls for pass ___
- Attack with quick approach and quick, shortened arm swing ___
- Attacker swings hitting arm high as set target ___

To Increase Difficulty
• Pass lower to the setter.

To Decrease Difficulty
• Pass higher to the setter.

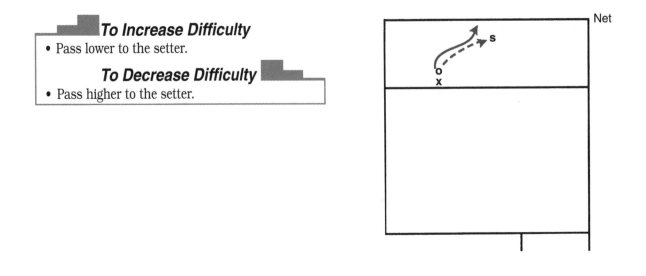

10. Setting a Bad Pass

The previous drills have all been based on a perfect pass to the setter. In this drill the setter practices moving to an imperfect pass and positioning to make a perfect set. The game philosophy of all players should be to always improve on the previous player's ball contact.

In a group of three players, one of you be the tosser, another the setter, and the third a target player. The tosser stands in the backcourt; the setter begins in the right back position; the target stands on the left sideline 1 to 2 feet off the net.

The tosser calls "go" and tosses the ball high and at least 10 feet away from the net, simulating an inaccurate pass. The setter has run to the setting position at the net on the signal "go." The setter reacts to the toss, moves off the net, squares shoulders to the left side of the court, and sets high outside to the target person. The set should be at least 7 feet higher than the net, and the target should not have to take more than one step to catch it.

Success Goal = 8 high, outside sets caught out of 10 attempts ___

Success Check
• Establish position before setting ball ___
• Setter's shoulders square to target ___
• Set ball 1 to 2 feet off net ___

To Increase Difficulty
• Toss lower to or farther from the setter.

To Decrease Difficulty
• Toss closer or higher to the setter.

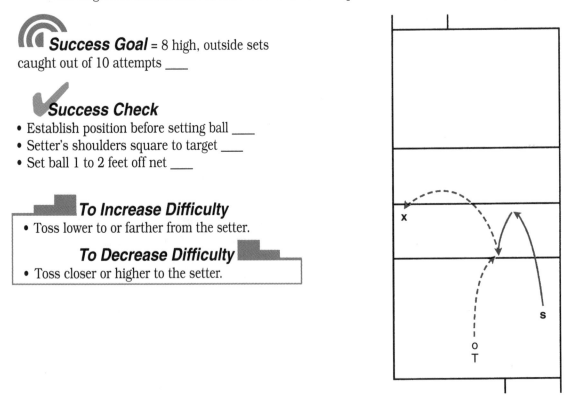

11. Serve, Forearm Pass, and Set

This drill simulates a game situation in which a player must receive a serve and pass it to a setter who has moved into the target area. The setter then sets a high outside ball to an attacker.

Assemble a group of four: a receiver in the left back position; a setter in the front at the net, at least 5 feet in from the right sideline; a target person just outside the left sideline; and, in the opposite court, a server in the service area (see Diagram a, below).

The server makes an underhand serve to the left back on the other side. The receiver forearm passes the ball to the setter, who should not have to move more than a step to play the ball. The setter sets the ball high outside, at least 6 feet higher than the top of the net and landing within a foot of the left sideline. The target person lets the ball bounce to check its accuracy, then returns it to the server.

Setter Option: When the receiver takes the serve in the right back position, the setter back sets the ball at least 5 feet higher than the net to within 1 foot of the right sideline (see Diagram b, below).

Success Goal =
12 legal serves out of 15 attempts ___
10 good forearm passes out of 12 attempts ___
8 good sets out of 10 attempts ___

Success Check
• Anticipate ___
• Call for ball before it crosses net ___
• Move, set, and cover ___

To Increase Difficulty
• Serve away from the receiver.
• Pass away from the setter.

To Decrease Difficulty
• Serve higher and with less force.
• Lengthen the time between serves.
• Serve directly at the receiver.
• Permit *only* an underhand serve.

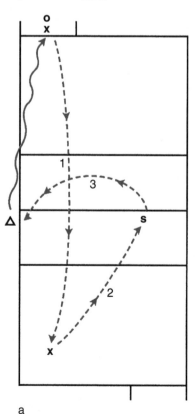

a

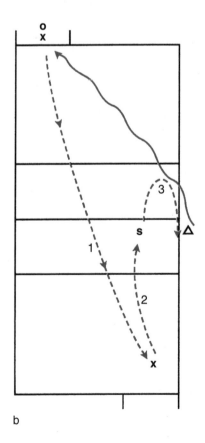

b

12. Reception Decision

This drill helps the two receivers begin to develop their decision making process of who should receive the serve. The two receivers are in positions similar to the deep positions used by many teams.

In a group of five, have a server in the service area of the court, two receivers on the opposite side in the back left and right halves, a setter in the front of the court at the net at least 5 feet in from the right sideline, and a target person standing just outside the left sideline.

The ball is served underhand alternately to each back quarter of the court. The receivers determine who will play the ball and call for it before it crosses the net. The ball is forearm passed to the setter who, as always, shouldn't have to move more than a step. The setter sets the ball high outside, at least 6 feet higher than the net and within 1 foot of the left sideline. The target person returns the ball to the server after letting it bounce.

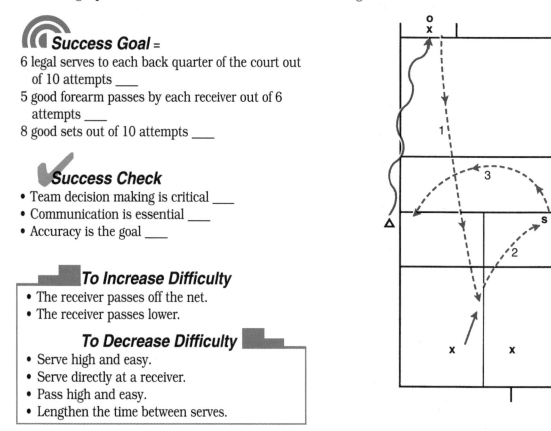

Success Goal =

6 legal serves to each back quarter of the court out of 10 attempts ___

5 good forearm passes by each receiver out of 6 attempts ___

8 good sets out of 10 attempts ___

Success Check

• Team decision making is critical ___
• Communication is essential ___
• Accuracy is the goal ___

To Increase Difficulty

• The receiver passes off the net.
• The receiver passes lower.

To Decrease Difficulty

• Serve high and easy.
• Serve directly at a receiver.
• Pass high and easy.
• Lengthen the time between serves.

13. Serve, Pass, and Set Game

This drill is competitive. It puts the players under gamelike pressure.

Teams of four players compete in this drill. Each team has its server on one side of the net and its forearm passer, setter, and target person on the opposite side of the net.

Both teams hit the balls at the same time. A team scores 1 point each time they complete the combination of a legal serve, a good forearm pass, and a good set. A legal serve is a serve that crosses the net without touching it and lands within the boundaries of the court. A good pass is any pass that allows the setter to set without moving more than one step in any direction. A good set is a ball that goes at least 6 feet higher than the net and lands on or within 1 foot of the left sideline. The target person catches the set after it bounces and returns it to the serving teammate on the opposite side.

Success Goal = be the first team to make 20 points ___

Success Check
- Call early for ball ___
- Receiver moves toward every serve ___
- Pass to setter 4 to 5 feet higher than net ___
- Setter calls for pass and indicates target ___

To Increase Difficulty
- Vary the type of serve.
- Server does not indicate target area to receiver.

To Decrease Difficulty
- Serve only underhand.
- Serve directly at the receiver.
- Increase size of target area for the pass or the set.

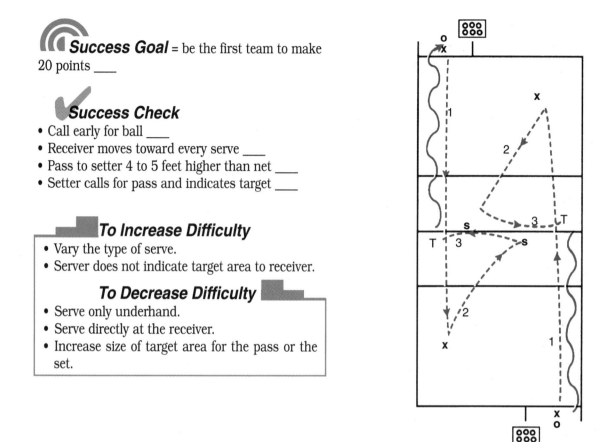

OVERHEAD PASS SUCCESS SUMMARY

You should feel confident in your ability to handle successfully any high, easy ball by using the overhead pass. Realize that the force imparted to the ball during execution uses your total body, especially when the pass needs to cover a large distance. Apply this force to the ball by extending your arms and legs and transferring your weight forward.

It is often said that an excellent setter makes an average attacker look good and an excellent attacker makes an average setter look good. You should be able to set the ball to the desired attack area regardless of the position of the pass. (Your job as a setter is made easier, of course, by excellent passing.) You must have a strong desire to set every ball well; set with the forearm pass only as a last resort.

When receiving a ball from the opponent, whether a serve, an attack, or a free ball, your team's goal is to receive the ball efficiently and to set your attack. You have now practiced the skills necessary to accomplish this transition. Have an instructor or another skilled volleyball player check your technique using the Keys to Success checklist in Figure 4.2.

STEP
5 ATTACK: MAKING THE KILL

You have been making kills efficiently and the opposing team is desperate to stop you. Your team receives a serve, makes an excellent pass, and the setter sets you a high outside set. The opponents are deep in the court and ready to dig another hard-driven spike. As you jump, you observe their defensive alignment and decide not to confront the block but to tip the ball along the net. The attack lands on the court for another kill.

There are three methods of attack in volleyball, each of which can be very effective. The first of the three methods to learn is the *tip*. It is often looked upon as a defensive maneuver to be performed when the conditions are not right for a more powerful attack. However, the tip is also an effective offensive technique since it disrupts the timing patterns of the defensive team.

The *off-speed spike* is a second option for the attacker. As indicated by its name, less than maximum force is imparted at contact. Like the tip, it is used to disrupt the timing patterns of the defensive team.

A third attack method is the *hard-driven spike*, the most exciting play in volleyball. It is also one of the most difficult of all sports skills to learn. To make a successful spike, you must jump into the air and sharply hit a moving object (the ball) over an obstacle (the net) so that it lands within a bounded area (the court). Due to the many variables associated with spiking, its timing is difficult and its success requires hours of practice.

When executing any attack, the position of the setter in relationship to the attacker is important. You hit the ball *on-hand* when the setter is on the same side as your hitting hand. This means that the set does not have to cross in front of your body before you make contact. If you are right-handed, you hit on-hand when in the left forward position; if left-handed, you hit on-hand when in the right forward position.

You attack the ball *off-hand* when the setter is on the opposite side from your hitting hand. If right-handed, you hit an off-hand spike when in the right forward position; if left-handed, you hit an off-hand spike when in the left forward position.

Why Is the Attack Important?

The attacking team should have many options. When your opponents have mastered the timing of your power attack, the tip can catch them off guard. It is much more difficult to cover the court defensively when a team mixes the speed of their attack. A well-placed tip often "breaks the back" of the opposition and may help improve the momentum of the offense.

The off-speed spike is similar in effect to the tip, but it is hit deeper into the opponent's court. When the off-speed spike is executed, placement rather than power is emphasized. The attacker hopes to force the defensive player to move from the starting defensive position and make an error in attempting to play the ball.

The hard-driven spike is the primary offensive weapon in volleyball. Most teams gain a majority of their points on successful spikes. The spike takes very little time to travel from the attacker's hand to the floor; therefore, there is little time for defensive players to move to the ball, and the defensive team must locate its players on the court in strategic positions before the ball is contacted on the spike.

Whichever attack you utilize, it should be easier for you to perform from your on-hand side. Also, your hard-driven spike is more powerful from the on-hand side.

The off-hand attack is important due to the rotation of positions in volleyball; you are required to attack efficiently from both sides of the court. Off-hand and on-hand considerations often determine the lineup. A coach would like to have the left-handers specialize as right-side attackers and the right-handers specialize as left-side attackers.

After learning the attack, you will have the skills necessary to complete the three-part sequence of forearm pass, set, and attack. The purpose of this sequence is to convert the opponent's attack or serve into your own attack. This conversion is referred to as a *transition*. After you receive your opponent's serve by cushioning it and passing it high to your setter, the setter places the ball in position for the attack. There are several types of sets, which are usually classified according to their placement and height. However, for the purposes of this first step—combining the three parts of the sequence—use only high outside sets.

Your team must be able to receive your opponent's serve and quickly and efficiently change from defense to offense. If your team is unable to make this transition, you will be forced to return a free ball to your opponent. A *free ball* is any ball that is returned over the net in a manner other than an attack. A free ball is easy to receive by the opponent, who can quickly gain an advantage by making a perfect pass and completing the transition into their own attack. Teams that are continually forced to return free balls to their opponent find themselves constantly on defense.

Attack Approach

The approach to all three types of attack is the same. For a high set, you, the attacker, begin on the attack line, wait for the set to be half the distance to you from the setter, and then move toward the set. Approach the net, covering the distance with as few steps as possible. The last two steps are the most important. Make a two-footed takeoff by planting your right foot heel first and closing with your left foot (bringing the left foot to a position even with the right foot) or by taking a hop onto both feet. As you plant both feet heels first to change forward momentum into upward momentum, swing your arms to prepare for a jump. Swing both arms forward and reach high toward the set as you jump straight up into the air. Draw your hitting arm back, your elbow high and your hand close to your ear. As you swing at the ball, drop your nonhitting hand quickly to your waist.

How to Execute the Tip

At contact gently direct the ball by using the upper two joints of the fingers of your hitting hand, slightly in front of your hitting shoulder at full arm extension. Contact the ball slightly below the center back. Direct the ball upward to barely clear the block but still drop quickly to the floor. Return to the floor with a two-footed landing (see Figure 5.1).

How to Execute the Off-Speed Spike

At contact in the off-speed spike, hit the ball with the heel of an open hand cutting into the center back of the ball. Immediately snap your wrist and roll your fingers over the top of the ball, imparting topspin, which causes the ball to drop. The follow-through is the same as for the tip (see Figure 5.2).

How to Execute the Hard-Driven Spike

In the hard-driven spike, contact the ball with the heel of an open hand cutting into the center back. At contact, forcibly snap your wrist and drop your arm toward your waist. The wrist snap imparts topspin, causing the ball to drop quickly to the floor. The follow-through is the same as for the off-speed spike (see Figure 5.3).

How to Execute On-Hand and Off-Hand

All attacks can be executed on-hand or off-hand. The only difference is the location of the ball in relation to your arm and body. When you perform on-hand (see Figure 5.4), contact the cross-court attack directly in front of your hitting shoulder and direct it toward the long diagonal part of the court. The down-the-line attack is contacted at the midline of your body.

When you perform off-hand (see Figure 5.5), contact the cross-court attack toward the midline of your body. In the down-the-line attack, contact the ball in front of your hitting shoulder. It is important that you recognize the difference between hitting on-hand and hitting off-hand. You must understand where the ball should be to successfully direct it either cross-court or down-the-line. For example, a right-handed left forward player hitting on-hand desires to make a down-the-line spike. If the player contacts the ball in front of the hitting shoulder instead of more toward the midline of the body, the spike will go toward the center back of the court.

FIGURE 5.1

KEYS TO SUCCESS

TIP

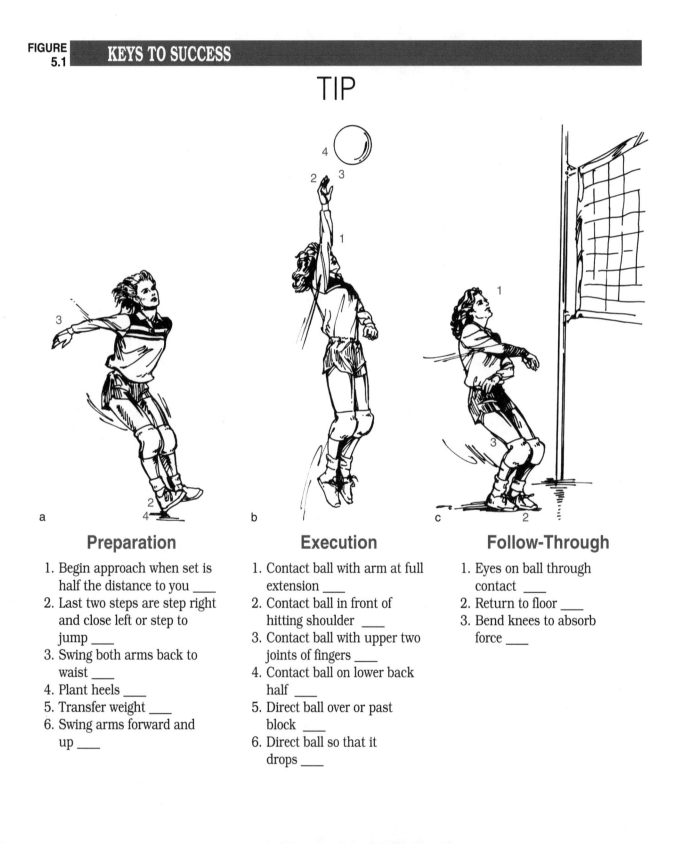

Preparation

1. Begin approach when set is half the distance to you ___
2. Last two steps are step right and close left or step to jump ___
3. Swing both arms back to waist ___
4. Plant heels ___
5. Transfer weight ___
6. Swing arms forward and up ___

Execution

1. Contact ball with arm at full extension ___
2. Contact ball in front of hitting shoulder ___
3. Contact ball with upper two joints of fingers ___
4. Contact ball on lower back half ___
5. Direct ball over or past block ___
6. Direct ball so that it drops ___

Follow-Through

1. Eyes on ball through contact ___
2. Return to floor ___
3. Bend knees to absorb force ___

FIGURE 5.2 **KEYS TO SUCCESS**

OFF-SPEED SPIKE

a   b   c

Preparation

1. Begin approach when set is half the distance to you ___
2. Last two steps are step right and close left or step to jump ___
3. Swing both arms back to waist ___
4. Plant heels ___
5. Transfer weight ___
6. Swing arms forward and up ___

Execution

1. Contact ball with arm at full extension ___
2. Contact ball in front of hitting shoulder ___
3. Contact ball with heel of hand ___
4. Contact ball on lower back ___
5. Roll fingers over top of ball ___
6. Flex wrist as fingers roll ___

Follow-Through

1. Eyes on ball through contact ___
2. Return to floor ___
3. Bend knees to absorb force ___
4. Drop hand to hip ___

FIGURE 5.3

HARD-DRIVEN SPIKE

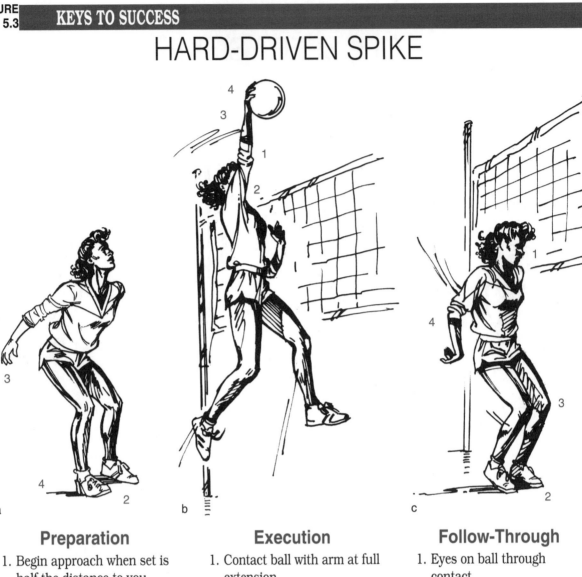

Preparation

1. Begin approach when set is half the distance to you ___
2. Last two steps are step right and close left or step to jump ___
3. Swing both arms back to waist ___
4. Plant heels ___
5. Transfer weight ___
6. Swing arms forward and up ___

Execution

1. Contact ball with arm at full extension ___
2. Contact ball in front of hitting shoulder ___
3. Contact ball with heel of open hand ___
4. Contact ball on center back ___
5. Snap your wrist forcibly ___
6. Direct hand over top of ball ___

Follow-Through

1. Eyes on ball through contact ___
2. Return to floor ___
3. Bend knees to absorb force ___
4. Drop hand forcibly to hip ___

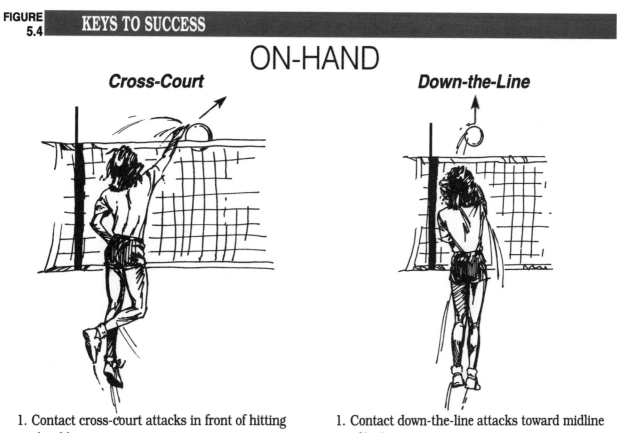

FIGURE 5.4 **KEYS TO SUCCESS**

ON-HAND

Cross-Court

Down-the-Line

1. Contact cross-court attacks in front of hitting shoulder ___

1. Contact down-the-line attacks toward midline of body ___

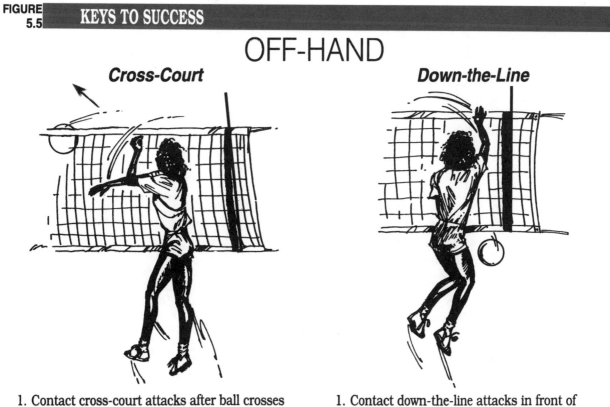

FIGURE 5.5 **KEYS TO SUCCESS**

OFF-HAND

Cross-Court

Down-the-Line

1. Contact cross-court attacks after ball crosses midline of body ___

1. Contact down-the-line attacks in front of hitting shoulder ___

ATTACK SUCCESS STOPPERS

Two common errors in executing the attack are (a) beginning the approach too soon and (b) contacting the ball behind the hitting shoulder. If you approach the ball too soon, two results are possible: (a) you have to stop, wait for the set, and thus lose the benefit of the approach; or (b) you have to back up to attack the ball because you have approached too far.

Most tip errors are associated with improper hand position in relation to the ball and poor timing during the approach. The off-speed spike is often referred to as a *roll shot*. This is because your hand rolls over the top of the ball as you flex the wrist. Balls contacted behind the hitting shoulder during the hard-driven spike consistently go out-of-bounds.

ERROR	CORRECTION
1. The ball goes into the net on a tip, an off-speed spike, or a hard-driven spike.	1. Contact the ball just in front of your hitting shoulder; the greater the distance the ball is in front of you, the lower it drops before contact and the greater the chance of its being hit into the net.
2. On a tip or off-speed spike, the ball does not clear the block.	2. Make contact on the back lower half of the ball with your arm fully extended.
3. On a tip, off-speed spike, or hard-driven spike, you stop your approach and wait for the ball.	3. Do not begin your approach until the ball is half the distance to you from the setter.
4. You contact the net during a tip or an off-speed spike.	4. The set must be at least 1 foot from the net; you must execute a heel plant to change horizontal momentum into vertical momentum.
5. On a tip or an off-speed spike, you hit the ball too high, and it takes too long to hit the floor.	5. Contact the ball in front of your hitting shoulder.
6. On a tip, off-speed spike, or hard-driven spike, the ball does not stay within 2 feet of the sideline and parallel to it in the down-the-line attack.	6. When you hit on-hand, the ball must pass your hitting shoulder and be contacted more toward the midline of your body. When you hit off-hand, the ball crosses the midline of your body and is contacted in front of your hitting shoulder.
7. Off your tip, the ball does not go diagonally along the net to the middle of the court. Off your off-speed spike, the ball does not go toward the center of the court close to the attack line.	7. When hitting on-hand, you should hit the ball in front of your hitting shoulder. When hitting off-hand, you should hit the ball after it crosses the midline of your body.
8. Off your hard-driven spike, the ball goes out-of-bounds over the end line.	8. You *must* contact the ball in front of your hitting shoulder; your wrist snaps your hand over the top of the ball.
9. You lack height on the jump during your hard-driven spike.	9. You must plant your heels to convert horizontal momentum into vertical momentum; both arms must swing forcibly upward.

ERROR	CORRECTION
10. You prepare for a hard-driven spike, but the set goes by you.	10. You must wait at the attack line until you know where the set will be.

ATTACK

DRILLS

1. Tip to Target Drill

This drill allows you to practice tipping to the two areas of the opponent's court that are usually most vulnerable during competition. The better area to choose would be based on your opponent's defensive alignment. A tip over the block and in front of the attack line is more successful against a 2-4 defensive system; a tip along the net toward the center of the court is more effective against the 2-1-3 defensive system.

This drill requires a group of three players—you as attacker starting at the attack line, another at the net as the setter, and the third standing on a chair on the opposite side of the net as a blocker. A 5-foot-wide target is located on the floor directly behind the blocker from the centerline to the attack line. A second target, 10 feet wide, is between the centerline and the attack line, beginning 10 feet from the sideline.

The setter tosses the ball high to the outside of the court. You approach and tip over the blocker's hands, which are extended over the top of the net. During your practices as attacker, tip onto each target.

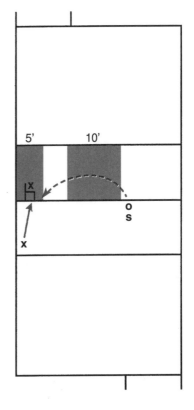

Success Goal =

5 tips landing in the 5-foot wide target area out of 10 tosses ___

5 tips landing in the 10-foot wide target area out of 10 tosses ___

Success Check

• Disguise approach ___
• Arm fully extended ___
• Direct ball to target ___
• Land on both feet ___

To Increase Difficulty

• Reduce the size of the targets.
• Use a two-person block.

To Decrease Difficulty

• Enlarge the targets.
• Do not use a blocker.
• The setter stands closer to the attacker.

2. Off-Speed Spike to Center Court

In this drill you practice placing the ball to another vulnerable area of the opponent's court. If placed in an open area, the off-speed spike is usually effective because of its change in speed.

This is almost the same as the previous drill. Your target here is a 10-foot square placed 5 feet from the net (extending 10 feet toward the end line). Place the target starting 10 feet in from each sideline.

As attacker, hit off-speed spikes over the blocker and onto the target from both the left and right sides.

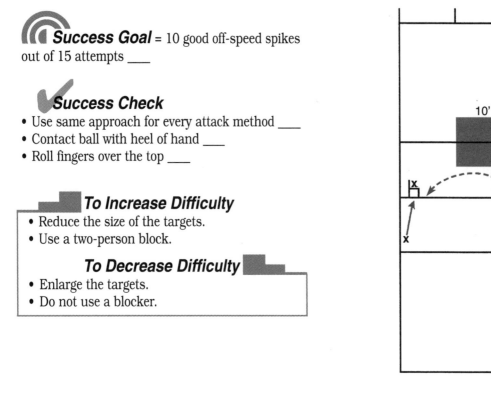

 **Success Goal** = 10 good off-speed spikes out of 15 attempts ___

✔ **Success Check**
• Use same approach for every attack method ___
• Contact ball with heel of hand ___
• Roll fingers over the top ___

To Increase Difficulty
• Reduce the size of the targets.
• Use a two-person block.

To Decrease Difficulty
• Enlarge the targets.
• Do not use a blocker.

3. Spike Hit Against Wall

This drill helps you to practice control contacting the top of the ball to direct it downward.

Stand by yourself with a ball 10 feet away from a wall. Spike the ball on an angle so that it contacts the floor about 5 feet in front of you. The ball should bounce sharply off the floor, rebound off the wall, and come back to you on the fly. Spike the ball again and continuously.

 **Success Goal** = 25 consecutive sharp spike hits ___

✔ **Success Check**
• Snap your wrist with arm fully extended ___
• Hit ball hard into floor___
• Follow through by snapping arm to waist ___
• Position for a rebound off wall ___

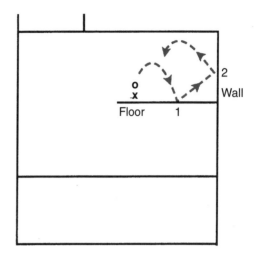

To Increase Difficulty
• Stand farther from the wall.

To Decrease Difficulty
• Stand closer to the wall.
• Place a mark on the floor to indicate the ideal ball contact spot.

4. Spike Hit for Direction

The corners of the court are usually the more vulnerable areas of your opponent's defense. This drill allows you to practice the correct body and shoulder position needed to direct the ball into one of the back corners of the court.

With a partner, you begin as a spiker at the attack line near either sideline. Your partner is a setter near the net. Mark two 10-foot-square target areas in the back corners of the opponent's court.

Pass the ball high to your partner. Your partner sets the ball back to you. Without jumping, spike hit the ball over the net to either of the two large target areas.

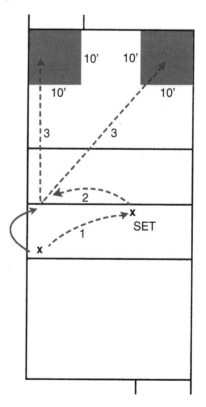

Success Goal =
5 spike hits out of 10 landing in the left back target area ___
5 spike hits out of 10 landing in the right back target area ___

Success Check
• Square shoulders to target ___
• Get to ball ___
• Hit at full extension ___
• Snap hand over ball to impart topspin ___

To Increase Difficulty
• Decrease the size of the target areas.

To Decrease Difficulty
• Enlarge the target areas.

5. Approach and Throw

This drill allows you to practice the correct approach and body position for any attack.

With a partner on the other side of the net, begin with a ball at the attack line. Approach the net carrying the ball, jump, and throw the ball forcibly over the net using a two-hand overhead motion with a wrist snap. Attempt to hit the front two thirds of the court. Your partner retrieves the ball and rolls it back to you.

Success Goal = 10 good tosses out of 15 attempts ___

Success Check
• Snap the wrist ___
• Square shoulders to target ___
• Hit floor as close to net as possible ___

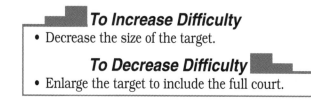

To Increase Difficulty
• Decrease the size of the target.

To Decrease Difficulty
• Enlarge the target to include the full court.

6. Bounce and Spike

In this drill you practice positioning your body for the attack based upon the position of the ball. This is gamelike in that the hitter should always approach the high set based on its location.

You and a partner set up as in the previous drill. Beginning at the attack line, bounce the ball forcibly into the floor, jump, and spike the rebound over the net. The ball must land within the boundaries of the opponent's court. Your partner retrieves the ball and rolls it back to you.

Success Goal = 10 good spikes out of 15 bounces ___

Success Check
• Bounce ball so that it rebounds straight up ___
• Get to ball before jumping ___
• Hit ball forcibly and with wrist snap ___

To Increase Difficulty
• Set up specific targets for the attacker to spike toward.

To Decrease Difficulty
• Lower the success goal.

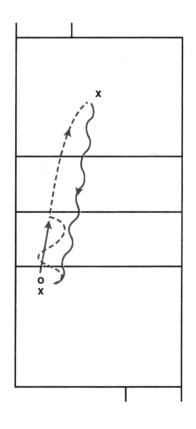

7. Spike Hits to the Corners

In this drill you practice directing the ball with a spike but without jumping off the court. Right-handers can practice from both their on-hand and off-hand sides.

With a partner near the net as a setter, you be a spiker at the attack line near either sideline. Place two 10-foot-square targets in the back corners of the opponent's court.

Pass the ball high to the setter. The setter sets the ball back to you. Without jumping, spike the ball over the net to either of two large target areas.

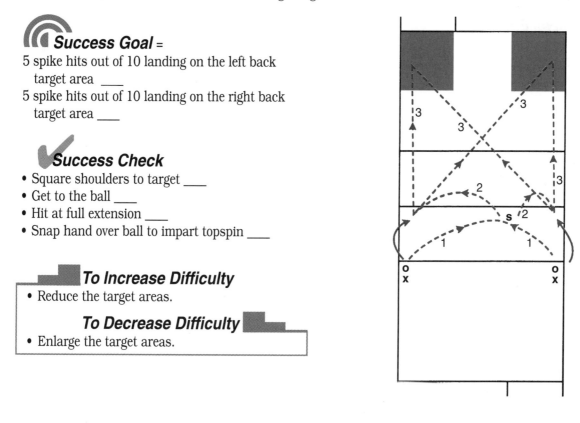

Success Goal =

5 spike hits out of 10 landing on the left back target area ____

5 spike hits out of 10 landing on the right back target area ____

Success Check

- Square shoulders to target ____
- Get to the ball ____
- Hit at full extension ____
- Snap hand over ball to impart topspin ____

To Increase Difficulty

- Reduce the target areas.

To Decrease Difficulty

- Enlarge the target areas.

8. Spiking From a Set

In this drill you will practice spiking down-the-line and cross-court from the left forward position on the court. Right-handers will be practicing on-hand spiking. Left-handers will be practicing off-hand.

Get together a group of four: a tosser on one side of the net and a receiver, a setter, and an attacker on the opposite side. Set up a 2-foot-wide target parallel to the right sideline.

The tosser throws the ball hard over the net to the receiver, who is standing in the backcourt. The receiver forearm passes the ball to the setter at the net right of center front, who sets the ball high outside along the net for the attacker waiting at the attack line. The attacker should try spiking the ball over the net both down-the-line into the target and cross-court into the back one-third corner of the opponent's side.

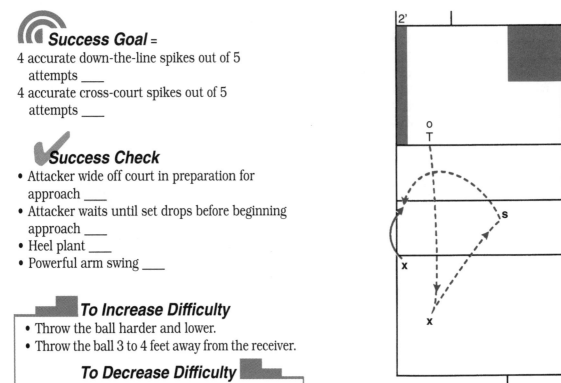

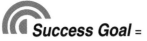 **Success Goal** =

4 accurate down-the-line spikes out of 5
  attempts ___
4 accurate cross-court spikes out of 5
  attempts ___

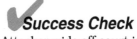 **Success Check**

• Attacker wide off court in preparation for
  approach ___
• Attacker waits until set drops before beginning
  approach ___
• Heel plant ___
• Powerful arm swing ___

To Increase Difficulty

• Throw the ball harder and lower.
• Throw the ball 3 to 4 feet away from the receiver.

To Decrease Difficulty

• Throw the ball easier and higher.
• Throw the ball directly at the receiver.

9. Spiking From a Back Set

In this drill you will practice down-the-line and cross-court spiking from the right forward position. Right-handers will be practicing their on-hand attacking. Left-handers will practice off-hand.

This is the same as the previous drill, with the following exceptions: The setter is right of center front and must back set the ball at least 5 feet higher than the net to the attacker, who must be at the attack line on the right sideline.

Success Goal =

4 accurate down-the-line spikes out of 5
  attempts ___
4 accurate cross-court spikes out of 5
  attempts ___

Success Check

• Attacker wide off court in preparation for
  approach ___
• Attacker waits until set drops before beginning
  approach ___
• Heel plant ___
• Powerful arm swing ___

To Increase Difficulty
- Throw the ball harder and lower.
- Throw the ball 3 to 4 feet away from the receiver.

To Decrease Difficulty
- Throw the ball easier and higher.
- Throw the ball directly at the receiver.

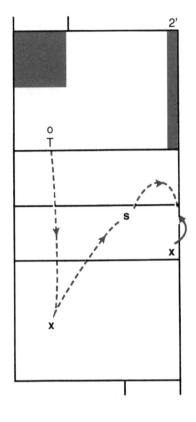

10. Pressure Spiking

In this drill you are put in a pressure situation of having little time to prepare for your approach. It simulates a game situation where you spike, are blocked, and immediately are set again.

Have three spikers line up one behind the other at the attack line on the left sideline. A tosser stands at the net, and additional players are needed as ball retrievers and feeders for the tosser.

The tosser continuously tosses balls high to the sideline. The first player approaches, spikes, and returns to the end of the line by making a circle in the clockwise direction. The second player immediately follows and spikes, followed by the third player. Action is continuous with minimal time between tosses until 30 tosses have been made. Retrievers and feeders must get balls back to the tosser quickly.

This drill can be executed by using either a down-the-line spike or a cross-court spike to a 10-foot-square target in the opposite corner of the court. The spikers should practice approaching from both sidelines.

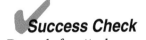 **Success Goal** = 10 good spikes by the group into the designated target out of 30 attempts ___

Success Check
- Be ready for attack every time ___
- Attack with force ___
- Recover quickly after attack ___

To Increase Difficulty
- Set the ball lower.
- Shorten the time between sets.

To Decrease Difficulty
- Set the ball higher.
- Lengthen time between sets.
- Increase the number of spikers.

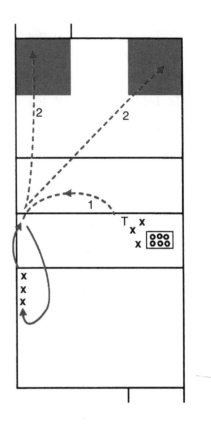

11. Serve, Forearm Pass, Set, and Attack

In this drill you are working as a team to receive your opponent's serve and convert it to an offense on your side of the net. You need a group of four players. One serves from the service area on one side of the court. On the other side, you have a receiver in the left or right back position; a setter in the front court at the net, at least 5 feet in from the sideline; and an attacker standing on the attack line at the sideline on the same side as the receiver.

The ball is served underhand to the receiver, who accurately forearm passes the ball to the setter. The setter sets the ball to the attacker at least 6 feet higher than the net, if forward (at least 5 feet higher than the net, if back) and within 1 foot of the sideline. The attacker hits the ball over the net using any one of the three attacks.

Success Goal =

12 legal serves out of 15 attempts ___
10 accurate forearm passes out of 12 attempts ___
8 good sets out of 10 attempts ___
5 successful attacks out of 8 attempts ___

Success Check
- Receiver calls for ball ___
- Passes as accurate as possible ___
- Set high and slightly off net ___
- Attack approach begins when set reaches highest point ___

To Increase Difficulty
- Use an overhand floater serve.
- Serve away from the receiver.

To Decrease Difficulty
- Serve ball higher.
- Serve with little force.
- Serve directly at the receiver.

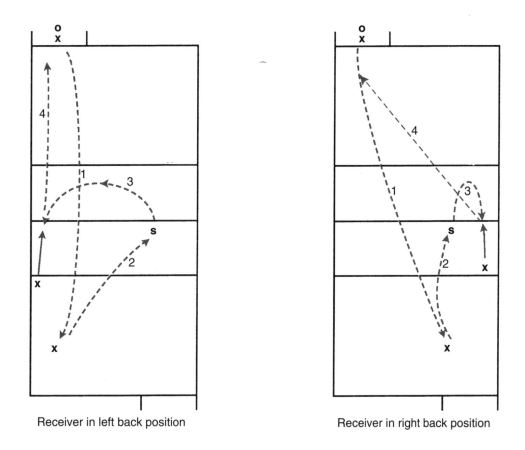

Receiver in left back position   Receiver in right back position

12. Continuous Three-on-Three

This drill is competitive and continuous. It allows teams of three players to compete using regular volleyball rules. It is gamelike and players can begin to experience the strategy of best attack placement.

Three-player teams line up one behind the other on the end line of one side of the court. Each team has a volleyball. Another team begins on the court on the opposite side of the net without a ball.

The first team in line serves and runs out onto their court. The ball is rallied until play is over. The team winning the rally scores a point. The winning team position themselves on the far court. The players of the losing team return to the end of the line. The next team of three serves immediately, and the game continues.

The purpose of this game is to make it to the far side of the court and remain there as long as possible by winning rallies. On the reception of serve, the team must complete the three-hit combination—pass, set, and attack—for the rally to continue. After serve reception, the ball may be returned with less than three hits. No tips in front of the attack line are allowed.

Success Goal = be the first team to obtain an agreed-upon number of points ___

Success Check
- Call early for ball ___
- Pass ball high and easy ___
- Set ball high ___
- Cover for each other ___

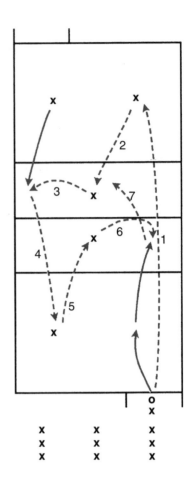

To Increase Difficulty

- Use teams of two players each.
- Vary the placement of the serve.
- Have a team receive a point only if they complete the three-hit combination, even after the initial service return.

To Decrease Difficulty

- Serve only underhand.
- Serve only to the back two thirds of the court.
- Increase the team size to four players.

13. Attack Line Tip Game

This is a competitive gamelike drill which forces players to be aware of their opponents' location on the court to make the best strategic decisions on placement.

Get together two teams of three each, one team on each side of the net. Play a game with the attack lines as the end lines.

Play is initiated with an overhead pass over the net. The receiving team must execute a three-hit combination of pass, set, and tip. The team that wins the rally wins a point. The team that loses the rally initiates the next rally with an overhead pass.

Success Goal = reach an agreed-upon number of points before your opponent ___

Success Check

- Call, move, set position for every ball ___
- Move to ball ___
- Set yourself ___
- Play ball ___
- Dig ball high ___
- Place ball to open area ___

To Increase Difficulty

- Enlarge the court area lengthwise and set up only one game on each court.
- Use two-person teams.

To Decrease Difficulty

- Use four-person teams.

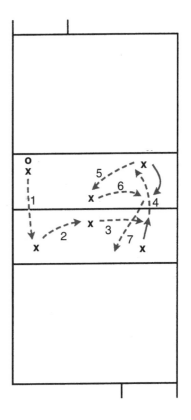

14. One-Third Court Game

This drill allows players to practice control and attack placement. Attacks will be straight ahead which simulates a down-the-line attack. It encourages the players to use the pass, set, and attack combination by giving more points for this achievement.

Place yourself and three other players into two teams of two each. Play a regular volleyball game, except that the court boundaries consist of the length of the court but only one third of its width.

Play is initiated by a serve from the end line. The rally continues until an error is made and a point is won. Two points are awarded for each three-hit combination. One point is awarded for winning a rally.

Success Goal = be the first team to earn a set number of points ____

Success Check

- Total communication ____
- Control and placement of attack ____
- Teamwork ____
- Read opponent's play ____

To Increase Difficulty

- The server may use a variety of serves.

To Decrease Difficulty

- Use three-person teams.
- The server uses only an underhand serve.
- Play only two games per court, using the two side thirds and allowing the players to move into the middle third to play the ball.

ATTACK SUCCESS SUMMARY

The attack in volleyball is one of the most difficult sports skills to perform. The most important element of good execution is proper timing. Beginners are often so anxious to complete the attack that they begin their approach much too early. You must watch the setter and follow the set to the highest point of its trajectory before initiating the approach.

When performing the tip, keep in mind that your attack must go over or by the opponent's block to be successful. Your body must be behind the ball so you can direct it to the most advantageous area of the opponent's court. Also, be aware that officials will usually call you for improper technique if you attempt to change the direction of the ball during tip performance. Attempting to change direction causes your hand to be in contact with the ball too long, and a held ball is called.

For successful hard-driven spikes, you need to concentrate on three areas of performance: (a) timing your approach, (b) keeping the ball in front of your hitting shoulder, and (c) forcibly snapping your wrist to impart topspin to the ball. Due to the complexity of the hard-driven spike, you should practice parts of the skill individually prior to putting them together. For example, you can approach and jump without using a ball.

Have another skilled volleyball player use the Keys to Success in Figures 5.1, 5.2, and 5.3 to evaluate your tip, off-speed spikes, and hard-driven spikes. Use the Keys to Success in Figures 5.4 and 5.5 to help recognize the difference between hitting on-hand and hitting off-hand.

Some coaches feel that the transition part of your game—receiving a serve or an attack from your opponent and converting it to your own attack—is the most important aspect of game strategy. It takes efficient play by two or three players for a successful transition to attack. Your team must make a good pass on serve reception, a good set, and a successful attack to put the opponent on defense. If there is a breakdown in any of these, the opponent will earn a point or a side out or receive a free ball for an easy transition.

STEP 6

INDIVIDUAL DEFENSIVE SKILLS:
NOTHING HITS THE FLOOR

The opponent has received your serve and made a perfect pass and set. The attacker leaves the floor with a powerful jump and is about to crush the ball. You are set in your defensive position outside the blocker's hand anticipating an awesome spike and hoping that you won't have the ball's brand name imprinted on your forehead. The ball is spiked past the block and directly at you. You place your forearm platform in the ball's path and pop it up perfectly to your setter. Your team is now ready to set its offense in transition.

The *dig* is the reception of the opponent's attack. It can be performed with either one or two hands. However, you should use a one-handed dig only in emergencies. When you dig with two hands, you have much more control and ability to direct the ball. Many people believe the spike is the most exciting part of volleyball, but it is the dig that generates the greatest amount of fan appeal. A match in which two evenly matched teams continuously dig the opponent's spikes creating long rallies is exciting to watch.

The essential element for successful digging is reading the opponent's attack to gain clues as to the direction of the upcoming spike or tip. A hard-driven spike travels so fast that it takes less than a half second to hit the floor. You must be in the correct defensive position to play the ball before the spike is made because there is not enough time to move after the ball is hit.

Two additional skills needed for individual defense are the roll and the sprawl. The *roll* is the preferred method because it allows you to return to your feet more quickly than the sprawl. The roll is used to recover when your body contacts the floor after digging the ball. It is similar to a forward roll and is done in such a way that padded body parts (those protected with extra layers of muscle) cushion your contact with the floor. The roll is not a method of digging, but rather a method of recovery.

The *sprawl* is a recent defensive technique probably coming into existence because players lack the strength to execute the dive. Female players especially are often more comfortable executing the sprawl. It is used mostly to play a ball in front of you, but you can also use it to play balls to either side. Like other defensive techniques, you use the sprawl when you need to move quite a distance to play the ball. It is most frequently used to receive a spiked ball.

Why Are Individual Defensive Skills Important?

The dig is the only skill that can successfully be used to receive an attack. Players use other skills in emergency situations but generally with limited success. Strong digging not only has great spectator appeal, but also tends to frustrate powerful spikers. If the attack is consistently dug, attackers begin to feel that they must change their strategy, which often results in errors.

The rolling technique is important because it aids you in quickly returning to your feet. It is also a method of falling that allows you to cushion the landing; thus, it helps to prevent injury. You would be likely to use the roll after you have had to chase the ball from your starting defensive position some distance to either side.

The sprawl allows you to dig balls that under normal conditions would not be receivable. It also is an option for playing the ball without resorting to the dive, which is difficult for players who have weak arms. The sprawl allows you to dig the ball from a low posture, contacting the floor with a sliding motion, thereby defusing the force of impact and preventing injury.

Once you have learned to receive the ball using the various individual defensive skills, you are ready to practice changing from defense to offense by using the dig as the first contact. The transitional phase is important. If your team cannot return your opponent's attack by converting it into your own attack, you will constantly find yourselves returning free balls to your opponent. A free ball is easy to convert into an attack; therefore, your team will constantly be on the defensive.

How to Execute the Dig

The performance of the dig in volleyball is somewhat similar to that of the forearm pass. The main difference is that in the forearm pass, you have time to move, set your position, and play the ball. In the dig, however, you must react and play the ball with little time to strategically position yourself. When digging a ball, you should allow it to drop as low as possible, increasing the amount of time you have to play it. You must cushion the ball, absorbing the

force from a hard-driven spike, and direct it high and toward the general vicinity of the center of the court, making it easier for your setter to play it. You should flick your wrists or flex the elbows at contact to ensure height and to ensure that the ball will remain on your side of the net (see Figure 6.1). The dig is often combined with other defensive skills, such as the sprawl and the roll, to enhance recovery and prevent injury.

How to Execute the Roll

There are several different methods of performing the roll in volleyball. Current thought is that what is important is not the method of roll but the body position from which you execute it. The primary aspect to successful rolling is to get as close as possible to the ball, let it drop low, and dig close enough to the floor so that your body contact with the floor does not come from a great height.

The most common method of rolling is this: Let the ball drop to approximately 1 foot from the floor and then hit it high into the air. Contact the floor with your hips and thighs and roll onto your back, bringing your feet and legs over the shoulder on the opposite side of your body from where you hit the ball. Then roll back up onto your feet. You can also execute the roll with your feet going over your head or by rolling side to side on your back. You should be able to roll to either side. Determine which methods of rolling feel most comfortable (see Figure 6.2).

FIGURE 6.1 **KEYS TO SUCCESS**

DIG

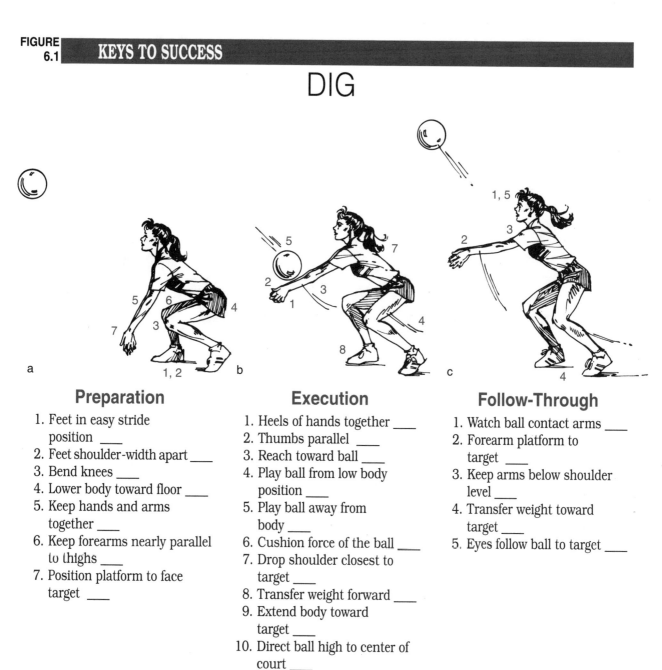

Preparation

1. Feet in easy stride position ___
2. Feet shoulder-width apart ___
3. Bend knees ___
4. Lower body toward floor ___
5. Keep hands and arms together ___
6. Keep forearms nearly parallel to thighs ___
7. Position platform to face target ___

Execution

1. Heels of hands together ___
2. Thumbs parallel ___
3. Reach toward ball ___
4. Play ball from low body position ___
5. Play ball away from body ___
6. Cushion force of the ball ___
7. Drop shoulder closest to target ___
8. Transfer weight forward ___
9. Extend body toward target ___
10. Direct ball high to center of court ___
11. Flick wrist(s) to gain height ___
12. Flex elbows to gain height ___

Follow-Through

1. Watch ball contact arms ___
2. Forearm platform to target ___
3. Keep arms below shoulder level ___
4. Transfer weight toward target ___
5. Eyes follow ball to target ___

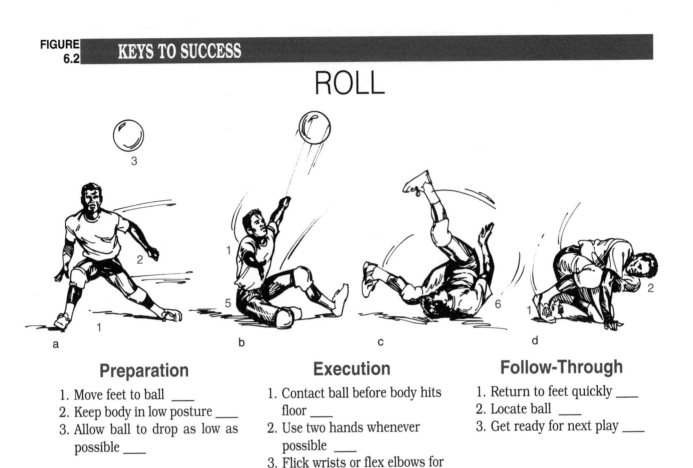

FIGURE 6.2 **KEYS TO SUCCESS**

ROLL

Preparation

1. Move feet to ball ___
2. Keep body in low posture ___
3. Allow ball to drop as low as possible ___

Execution

1. Contact ball before body hits floor ___
2. Use two hands whenever possible ___
3. Flick wrists or flex elbows for height ___
4. Direct ball to center of court ___
5. Contact floor with padded body parts ___
6. Roll to spread force of contact ___

Follow-Through

1. Return to feet quickly ___
2. Locate ball ___
3. Get ready for next play ___

How to Execute the Sprawl

In a low body position and with your feet in a wide stride, one foot ahead of the other, let the ball drop to about a 1-foot height, reach for the ball, and dig it high to the middle of the court. Continue to move forward, contacting the floor with your arms and chest in a sliding action. Extend your back leg be-hind you while you bend your front leg at the knee and keep it out to the side, the side of the knee con-tacting the floor (see Figure 6.3).

It is more difficult to return to your feet after ex-ecuting a sprawl than after executing a roll. You can make a similar sliding action with your body on its side, particularly after a dig using one hand.

FIGURE
6.3 **KEYS TO SUCCESS**

SPRAWL

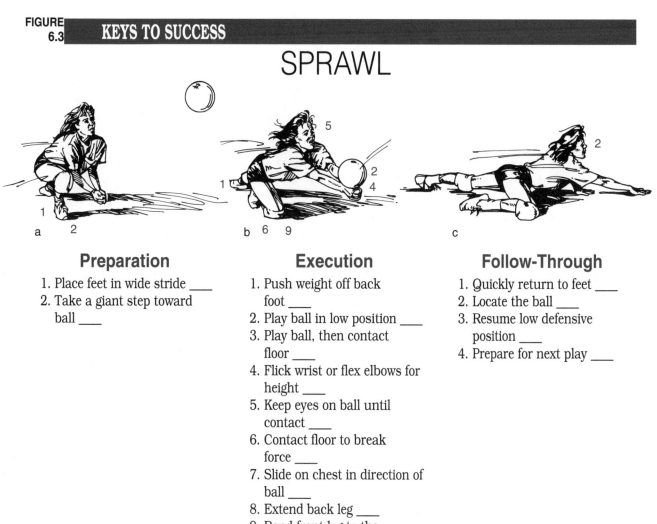

a   2   b   6   9   c

Preparation

1. Place feet in wide stride ___
2. Take a giant step toward ball ___

Execution

1. Push weight off back foot ___
2. Play ball in low position ___
3. Play ball, then contact floor ___
4. Flick wrist or flex elbows for height ___
5. Keep eyes on ball until contact ___
6. Contact floor to break force ___
7. Slide on chest in direction of ball ___
8. Extend back leg ___
9. Bend front leg to the outside ___
10. Contact floor with inside of knee ___

Follow-Through

1. Quickly return to feet ___
2. Locate the ball ___
3. Resume low defensive position ___
4. Prepare for next play ___

INDIVIDUAL DEFENSIVE SKILLS SUCCESS STOPPERS

The greatest cause for dig errors is a poor beginning defensive position. As a backcourt defensive player, you must begin near the sidelines or end lines of the court. This helps you keep the ball in front of you and on the court. Every effort should be made to get both arms, or at least one arm, on the ball to keep it in play.

There are three major errors in performing the roll: (a) not getting low enough to the floor before digging the ball, (b) attempting to roll before the dig, and (c) contacting the floor with the wrong parts of the body

first. Roll errors should be corrected as soon as possible because they are likely to cause injury eventually.

With the sprawl, the contact of the ball can be on your forearm, your hand, or the back of your hand. You may use one or both arms, although using two is preferred because it allows more control. As with the roll, the greatest concern is to play the ball high to the middle of the court in the most efficient manner, while preventing injury.

ERROR	CORRECTION
Dig	
1. The ball goes straight up or back over your head.	1. Try to stop your arms on contact by using a "poking" action on the ball. Let the ball drop to waist level or lower before contact.
2. The ball is low and fast as it leaves your arms.	2. Bend your knees, keeping your back straight, as you move under the ball; touch the floor with your hands to stay in a low position.
3. You do not transfer your weight toward the intended target.	3. Check to see that your weight ends up on your forward foot and that your body is inclined forward.
4. The ball does not go high (2 or 3 feet above the net) and toward the center of the court.	4. To make the ball go high, flick your wrists or flex your elbows at contact.
5. The ball does not remain on your side of the net.	5. At contact, flick your wrists or flex your elbows.
6. The ball hits your arms and continues in the same direction it was already going.	6. Drop the shoulder closer to the target to change the platform angle so that it faces the target.
Roll	
1. You contact the floor hard, resulting in discomfort.	1. Take a large step toward the ball and assume as low a position as possible.
2. You contact the floor before hitting the ball.	2. You should complete the dig before the roll begins.
3. You take too long to return to your feet and are not ready for the next play.	3. Once the roll begins, make the action as quick as possible to get back on your feet.
4. You play the ball too high (more than 1 1/2-2 feet) above the floor.	4. The lower you let the ball drop, the better the dig.
Sprawl	
1. You play the ball at a height greater than 2 feet.	1. Take a big step toward the spot where the ball will be played, at the same time lowering your body.
2. You contact the floor before contacting the ball.	2. Contact the ball before the floor so that your hands are available to aid in breaking the fall.
3. You do not rapidly return to your feet.	3. You must quickly return to your feet and assume a low, defensive position.

DRILLS

1. Pepper

This drill gives you the opportunity to practice digging a hard-hit ball with control and height. With a partner, player A tosses the ball to himself or herself and spikes it toward player B. Player B digs the ball back to player A, who sets it to B. B then spikes the ball back to A, who digs it back to B. This nonstop action can continue indefinitely.

Success Goal = 5 digs within a nonstop sequence ____

Success Check
• Low body posture ____
• Platform to target ____
• Consistency ____

To Increase Difficulty
• Increase the force of the spike.
• Increase distance between partners.
• Direct the spike to either side of the digger.

To Decrease Difficulty
• Reduce the force of the spike.
• Decrease distance between partners.

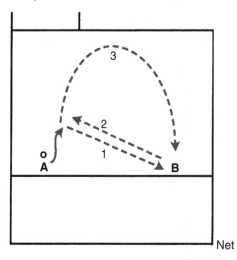

2. Digging Left Back, Middle Back, Right Back

This drill allows you to work on digging a spike in a more gamelike setting. The spiker does not use an approach, so you can concentrate on positioning yourself based on the shoulder position and arm swing of the spiker.

The location of this player simulates the left back, the middle back, and the right back defensive positions.

For the left back position, begin on the left sideline approximately 20 feet from the net with your back to the sideline. A partner stands on a box, chair, or official's stand in the left forward position on the opposite side of the net.

Your partner self-tosses and spikes the ball to you. You must dig the ball 2 to 3 feet higher than the top of the net and toward the center of the court. Repeat this drill with the digger in the middle back position just outside the end line, and again with the digger in the right back position, 20 feet from the net and on the right sideline.

Success Goal = 6 out of 10 successful digs in each position ____

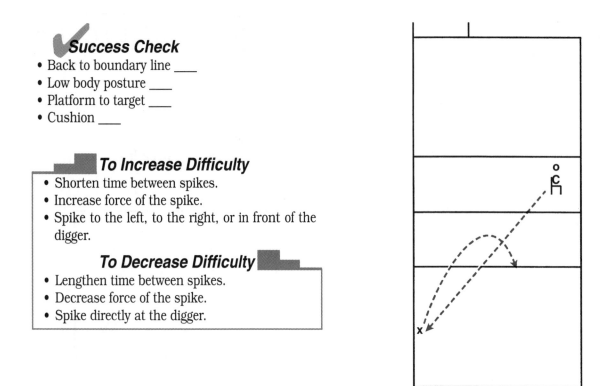

✔ Success Check

- Back to boundary line ____
- Low body posture ____
- Platform to target ____
- Cushion ____

▰ To Increase Difficulty

- Shorten time between spikes.
- Increase force of the spike.
- Spike to the left, to the right, or in front of the digger.

To Decrease Difficulty ▰

- Lengthen time between spikes.
- Decrease force of the spike.
- Spike directly at the digger.

3. Two-Person Digging

This drill simulates a game situation where two backcourt defensive players are working together to receive an attack that is directed between them. Both players must move toward the ball. The height and speed of the ball determines who should receive it.

With a partner as another defensive player, take starting positions in any of the following combinations: left back and center back, right back and center back, or left forward and left back.

Another partner, on the other side of the net as in the three previous drills, spikes the ball between your two defensive players. The defender closer to the net always crosses in front of the defender farther from the net as you both move to dig the ball.

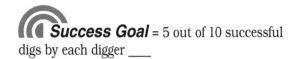 **Success Goal** = 5 out of 10 successful digs by each digger ____

✔ Success Check

- Call for ball ____
- Move through ball ____

To Increase Difficulty

- Shorten the time between spikes.
- Increase force of the spike.
- Direct some spikes toward the sidelines.

To Decrease Difficulty

- Lengthen time between spikes.
- Decrease force of the spike.
- Spike the ball closer to one player.

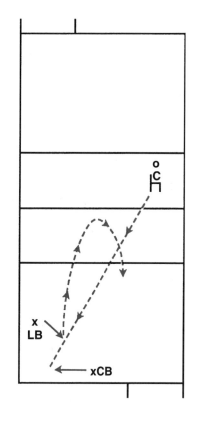

4. Roll Without a Ball

In this drill you practice rolling without having to play a ball first. This allows you to develop a level of comfort on hitting the floor.

Get into a low position, make sure that your padded body parts contact the floor first, and return to your feet as quickly as possible.

Success Goal = complete 10 rolls to either side ___

Success Check

- Long striding step ___
- Low body position ___
- Padded body parts contact floor ___
- Roll and quickly return to feet ___

To Increase Difficulty

- Increase distance to cover before rolling.

To Decrease Difficulty

- A partner helps you perform the skill.
- Begin in a low position.

5. Dig to Roll

In this drill you practice moving to a ball that is hit away from you. The easy toss allows you time to move and play the ball. This permits you to develop the skill of rolling before you need to receive a hard-driven spike.

Have a partner near the net, facing the end line. You stand in the left back position. Your partner tosses a low, easy ball alternately to either side of you. Let the ball drop low, dig the ball, and roll, quickly returning to your feet.

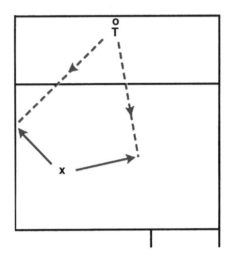

Success Goal =

5 successful dig-roll combinations out of 10 tosses to the right ____

5 successful dig-roll combinations out of 10 tosses to the left ____

Success Check

• Long striding step ____
• Low body position ____
• Play ball before contact with floor ____
• Ball drops as low as possible before contact ____
• Dig ball higher than top of net ____
• Direct ball back toward tosser ____

To Increase Difficulty

• Toss the ball farther from the digger.
• Toss the ball lower.

To Decrease Difficulty

• Toss the ball closer to the digger.
• Toss the ball higher.

6. Sprawl Without Ball

This drill allows you to become comfortable hitting the floor. It helps you to decrease the fear of injury often associated with the sprawl.

Working individually, practice the sprawling skill without a ball. Take a large step forward, slide forward as your body contacts the floor, and return to your feet as quickly as possible.

Success Goal =

5 sprawls forward ____
5 sprawls to the right ____
5 sprawls to the left ____

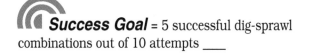

Success Check

- Long striding step forward ___
- Body as low to floor as possible ___
- Push off rear foot ___
- Slide on stomach and chest ___
- Bend one knee ___
- Reach forward with arm ___

To Increase Difficulty

- Cover more distance before sprawling.

To Decrease Difficulty

- Player begins on one knee.
- Practice on a smooth, nonstick surface.

7. Dig to Sprawl

This drill allows you to practice receiving a ball which is far in front of you. You must move quickly forward, dig the ball, and then sprawl as you recover.

Stand on the end line in the center back position. Have a partner near the net facing you. Your partner tosses a low ball so that it would drop 3 to 4 feet in front of you. Step forward, reach, and play the ball in a low position, digging it high to the center of the court and sprawling.

Success Goal = 5 successful dig-sprawl combinations out of 10 attempts ___

Success Check

- Long striding step toward ball ___
- Long slide to dissipate force ___
- Ball drops as low as possible ___
- Dig ball high ___
- "Break" wrists to improve dig height ___

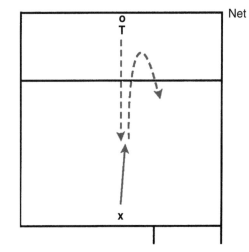

To Increase Difficulty

- The tosser makes the defensive player move a greater distance.
- The tosser throws the ball with more force.
- The defensive player must dig the ball to a specified height for it to be counted toward the Success Goal.

To Decrease Difficulty

- Toss the ball closer to the defensive player.
- The defensive player starts on one knee.

8. Roll or Sprawl Decision

This drill helps develop good decision making when you are receiving a ball on defense. Your choice of the correct defensive recovery skill is based on the location and direction of the oncoming ball. When movement is forward, the sprawl should be your choice. When moving to the sides, the roll is more appropriate. Remember, use the sprawl or roll only when it is absolutely necessary.

Stand in any of the defensive positions on the court. Have a partner stand at the net facing you. Your partner tosses the ball to either side of you or in front of you. You must decide which defensive skill to use, dig the ball, and execute the roll or sprawl correctly.

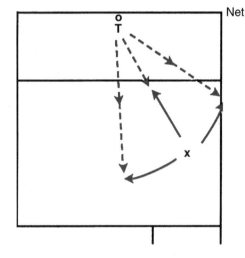

Success Goal = 5 correct defensive plays out of 10 attempts ___

✔ Success Check
• Quick movement and decision making ___
• Ball drops low before contact ___
• Contact ball before hitting floor ___
• Dig ball high and toward center of court ___

To Increase Difficulty
• Toss the ball with more force.
• Toss the ball farther from the defensive player.

To Decrease Difficulty
• Toss the ball closer to the defensive player.
• Toss the ball with less force.
• Tosser indicates the direction of the throw before tossing.

9. Spike Hit, Dig, Sprawl, or Roll

In this drill the ball you are receiving is hit with more force than in the previous drills. Remember the higher you dig the ball, the easier it is for a teammate to execute the next play.

Position yourself with a partner as in the previous drill. Your partner tosses the ball to himself or herself and spike hits it at you. Dig the ball higher than the height of the net to the center of the court; use a roll or sprawl when needed. Your partner catches the ball.

Success Goal = 7 successful digs out of 10 attempts ___

✔ *Success Check*

- Anticipate direction of ball and react ___
- Let ball drop low ___
- Dig ball high ___
- Recover quickly for next play ___

To Increase Difficulty

- Spike the ball lower.
- Spike the ball farther from the receiver.
- Spike the ball with greater force.

To Decrease Difficulty

- The spiker indicates the direction of the ball before spiking.
- Spike the ball with less force.
- Spike the ball higher.

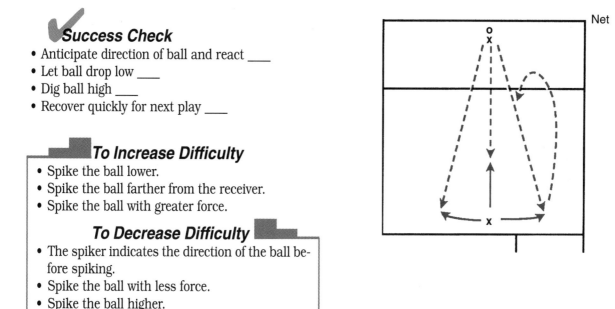

10. Spike, Dig, Roll, or Sprawl

In this drill you practice receiving a spike from an opponent. You need to watch the spiker's shoulders for clues as to the direction of the spiked ball. Remember to use a roll or a sprawl only if necessary to reach the ball. Stay on your feet if possible.

Get together a group of four players, two of you on offense and two on defense. On one side of the net, a setter stands close to the net, and a spiker starts at the attack line in the left front position. On the other side, one defensive player is positioned in the center back on the end line; the other defender stands on the left sideline, about 20 feet from the net.

On the offensive side, the setter sets the ball to the spiker, who spikes the ball on the diagonal to the left back quarter of the opponent's side. The defenders both move toward the ball, quickly deciding who should play it. One of them digs the ball, using a roll or sprawl if necessary.

The attackers receive a point for each spike not dug. The defensive players receive a point for each successful dig going higher than the top of the net and to the center of the court. A ball not spiked to the left back quarter of the opponent's side does not count.

🎯 *Success Goal* = be the first team to reach an agreed-upon number of points ___

✔ *Success Check*

- Watch arm of spiker ___
- Move toward ball and react ___
- Defensive player should not decide early who will play the ball ___
- Call for ball if time allows ___

To Increase Difficulty

- Spike with greater force.
- Spike the ball in any direction.

To Decrease Difficulty

- The spiker indicates the intended direction of the spike.
- The players practice one direction for a number of trials before changing the direction.
- Spike with less force.
- The spiker hits the ball directly at one of the defensive players.

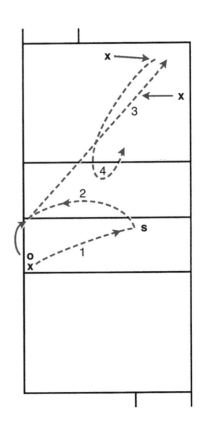

11. Serve, Forearm Pass, Set, Attack, and Dig

The drill is gamelike because it starts with serve reception and is followed by an attack that must be dug by a player on the opposite side of the net.

In a group of five, have a server and a digger on one court and a passer, a setter, and an attacker on the opposite court. The server underhand serves the ball to the passer, who is in the left back position of the other court. The passer forearm passes the ball to the setter, who shouldn't have to move more than a step. The setter sets high (at least 6 feet higher than the net) and outside to the attacker, positioned on the attack line at the left sideline. The attacker spikes the ball over the net to the left back area of the opponent's court. The digger plays the ball so that it is 2 to 3 feet higher than the top of the net and to the center of his or her own court.

Success Goal =

12 out of 15 legal serves ___
10 out of 12 good forearm passes ___
8 out of 10 good sets ___
6 out of 8 legal spikes ___
4 out of 6 good digs ___

Success Check

- Call for ball ___
- Pass with control ___
- Accurate set ___
- Vary speed of attacks ___

To Increase Difficulty
- Shorten the time between serves.
- Use an overhand floater serve.
- Increase the force of the serve.

To Decrease Difficulty
- Lengthen the time between serves.
- Decrease the force of the serve.
- Increase the trajectory of the serve.

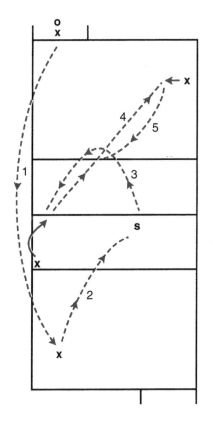

12. Serve, Forearm Pass, Back Set, Attack, and Dig

This drill is similar to the previous one except that the attack is from the right side of the court. The passer is in the right back position; the setter back sets the ball at least 5 feet above the top of the net and toward the right sideline; the attacker is positioned on the attack line at the right sideline; and the digger is in the right back position.

Success Goal =

12 out of 15 legal serves ____
10 out of 12 good forearm passes ____
8 out of 10 good sets ____
6 out of 8 legal spikes ____
4 out of 6 good digs ____

Success Check

- Call for ball ____
- Pass with control ____
- Accurate set ____
- Vary speed of attacks ____

To Increase Difficulty

- Shorten the time between serves.
- Use an overhand floater serve.
- Increase the force of the serve.

To Decrease Difficulty

- Lengthen the time between serves.
- Decrease the force of the serve.
- Increase the trajectory of the serve.

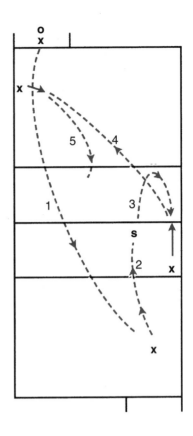

13. One Setter Three-on-Three

This is a competitive drill in which the rally continues under regular volleyball rules until an error is made. There is only one setter, however, who must set the attack for both teams. This drill gives the setter many contacts on the ball and lots of movement for conditioning.

For this drill you need three players on each side of the court—a server, a digger, and an attacker. A seventh player acts as a setter, alternating sides of the net, depending upon the location of the ball.

The game is initiated with a serve, and the ball is rallied, generally according to regular game rules. The setter, though, always assumes a position right of center front on the side of the court where the ball is being played, changing sides of the court as the ball goes over the net. The setter sets the hitters at the attack line to increase the other side's digging opportunities. The team winning a rally scores a point. The team losing the rally makes the next serve.

Success Goal = be the first team to reach a predetermined number of points ___

Success Check

- Read the position ___
- Prepare for attack ___
- Call for serve reception ___
- Vary the speed of attack ___

To Increase Difficulty

- Decrease the number of players per side.
- Use a variety of serves.
- Attack from any distance from the net.

To Decrease Difficulty

- Use only underhand serves.
- Use two setters instead of one.
- Add one or two attackers to each team.
- No tips may land in front of the attack line.

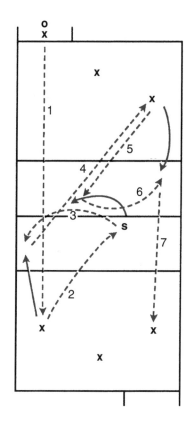

14. Diggers and Receivers

This drill allows each team to practice both setting an attack from serve reception and digging an attack for transition.

For this drill you need two teams of five players each on opposite sides of the net. Team A has a server, three diggers, and a setter. Team B has two serve receivers, two attackers, and a setter.

Team A serves; team B receives, setting up an attack with the set being made to the attack line. Team A digs the ball and sets at least 7 feet higher than the top of the net so that the ball lands on or within 1 foot of the left sideline (no further attack).

Team A serves 5 times, and then the two teams reverse roles. The receiving team gets 1 point for a successful attack, and the digging team gets 1 point for a successful dig and set.

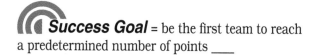 **Success Goal** = be the first team to reach a predetermined number of points ___

Success Check
- Read the opponent's attack ___
- Read the opponent's defense ___
- Call every ball ___
- Aggressively send ball to opponent ___

To Increase Difficulty

• Use a variety of serves.
• Attack from any distance from the net.

To Decrease Difficulty

• Use only an underhand serve.
• Enlarge the target area for the set.
• Allow no tips in front of the attack line.

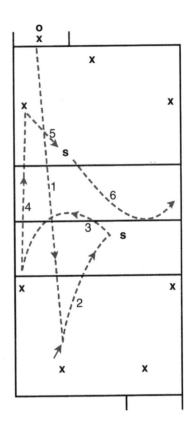

INDIVIDUAL DEFENSIVE SKILLS SUCCESS SUMMARY

To dig successfully you must read your opponent's attack. You should concentrate on the opposing attacker's approach, location of the set, position of the shoulders, and arm swing. All defensive players should use these observations to determine their best starting locations.

If the result of digging and rolling is a ball played high and to the middle of the court so that a teammate can set the attack, the play has been successful. The form of the roll is not critical as long as you prevent yourself from being injured and quickly return to your feet for the execution of the next play. Make sure that your body is in a low position close to the floor and that the ball is played before you attempt to execute a roll.

The essential aspect of a good sprawl is the large step toward the ball that allows you to assume a position low to the floor. The closer your body is to the floor, the easier it is to perform the sprawl and the less the chance of injury.

Another skilled volleyball player should use the criteria found in the Keys to Success Figures 6.1, 6.2, and 6.3 to assess your individual defensive skills.

STEP

7

BLOCKS: LIMITING THE OPTIONS

Your opponent has a powerful attacker in the left forward position. You are the blocker in the right forward position. The set is perfect and the attacker is making her approach. You set the block on her hitting hand and the middle blocker joins you to form a double block. You both jump together just after the attacker. Your arms penetrate over the net. The ball rebounds off your hands and back into the attacker's face. The attacker cannot react quickly enough and the rally ends in a point for your team.

The block is the first line of defense against your opponent's attack. The purpose of the block is to take a portion of your court away from the opponent. A block can be considered successful if the ball rebounds off the blocker's hands directly back into your opponent's court, if the blocker deflects the ball so that it goes high in the air on your team's side of the court, or if the block forces the opponent to direct its attack to a waiting defensive player on your team.

In a *single block*, only one player blocks at a time. Single blocking in volleyball is often not enough to stop the opposing attack. The purpose of the block is to take away as much court as possible from the attacker. Therefore, the wider the block, the less court the remaining defensive players must cover. Teams often join two or three players together, forming double or triple blocks, referred to as *multiple blocks*.

Once you have practiced the block, you have mastered the basic skills of volleyball and you can begin to move into gamelike situations. During the actual competition, one play sequence can include a serve, which is forearm passed to the setter, who sets to the attacker, who attempts to hit into the opponent's court, where the opponent defends with a block, a dig, or both. This sequence happens continually throughout a game.

Why Are Single and Multiple Blocks Important?

If your block prevents the ball from entering your side of the court, your opponent must set the attack a second time. This is important because the longer your opponent plays the ball, the greater the chance for error. Even though you deflect the ball into your own side of the court, if it is deflected high enough, the block is considered successful because it allows the defensive players behind you time to play a less forceful ball.

The greater the territory that can be eliminated from the attacker, the easier it is to defend the remaining court. If time allows players to get into position, you should always employ at least a double block. It is difficult to use a multiple block when defending the quick attack, which usually occurs near the middle of the court. Teams often use a single block in the middle of the court and a multiple block near the sidelines.

The sequence of serve, forearm pass, set, attack, and block or dig is the basis of the game of volleyball. Each time a team receives the ball from the opponent, it attempts to make the transition to offense with a forearm pass, a set, and an attack. At the same time, the opposing team is setting its defense, consisting of blocking and backcourt play. In order for the game to flow, teams must master this sequence of play.

How to Execute a Single Block

As the blocker, begin by standing within 1 foot of the net, facing the opposite court. Your hands are out to your sides at shoulder level, palms facing forward with fingers spread wide. Watching the opposing setter, wait until the ball is set to the hitter across the net from your position on the court, then change to watch the attacker until the ball comes into view. Attempt to line up one-half body width toward the opponent's hitting side.

Immediately after the attacker jumps, bend your knees and jump. Reach over the top of the net, your hands penetrating into your opponent's court, and position your hands to both sides of the attacker's hitting arm. Attempt to make the ball rebound off your hands back into the opponent's court. Return to the floor with a two-footed landing. Immediately turn off the net to locate the position of the ball (see Figure 7.1).

How to Execute Multiple Blocks

The execution of the double and triple blocks are similar to the execution of the single block. The main difference is that two or three players join together to block (see Figure 7.2). When the block is on the outside of the court, the outside player sets the block and the middle player joins the outside player. When moving to join the outside player, the middle player should watch the outside player moving to that position; then both players can jump at the same time. The outside player's hands are directly lined up with the ball, and the middle player's hands take away the cross-court angle.

When the middle blocker is blocking and the opponent's set is high enough, both outside players move to join the middle player, forming a triple block. During this block, the middle blocker's hands directly line up with the ball, and the outside blockers take away the angles.

FIGURE
7.1 **KEYS TO SUCCESS**

SINGLE BLOCK

a

b

c

Preparation

1. Focus on setter ____
2. After set, focus on attacker ____
3. Position one-half body width to attacker's hitting side ____
4. Wait with hands at shoulder level ____
5. Spread fingers ____
6. After setter contacts pass, bend knees and raise hands ____
7. Keep high position during movement ____

Execution

1. Jump just after attacker jumps ____
2. Penetrate into opponent's court ____
3. Withdraw hands ____
4. Return to floor ____
5. Land on two feet ____

Follow-Through

1. Bend knees to cushion landing ____
2. Turn away from net ____
3. Look for the ball ____
4. Return to original position ____
5. Prepare for next play ____

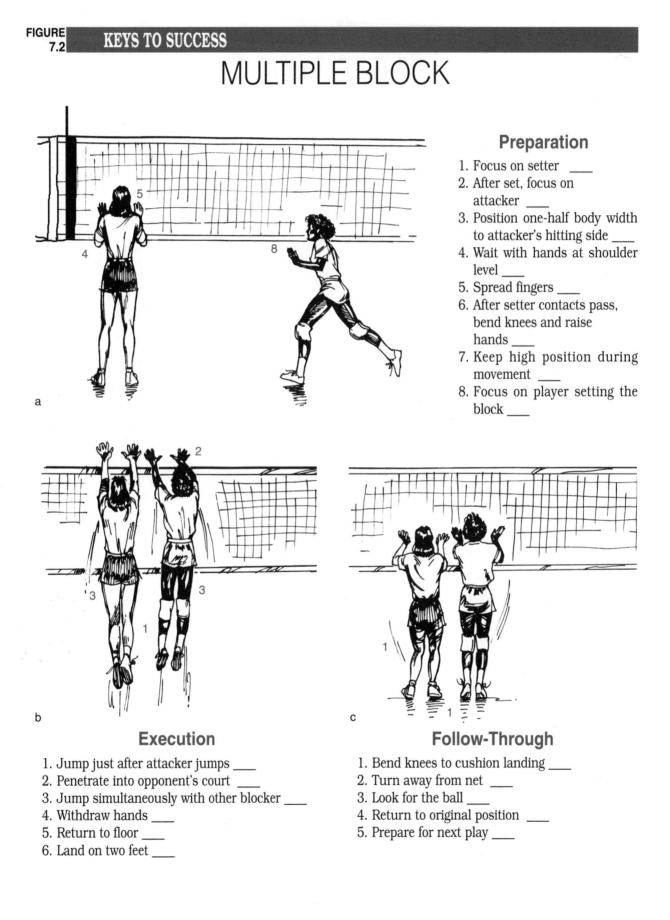

FIGURE 7.2

KEYS TO SUCCESS

MULTIPLE BLOCK

Preparation

1. Focus on setter ___
2. After set, focus on attacker ___
3. Position one-half body width to attacker's hitting side ___
4. Wait with hands at shoulder level ___
5. Spread fingers ___
6. After setter contacts pass, bend knees and raise hands ___
7. Keep high position during movement ___
8. Focus on player setting the block ___

Execution

1. Jump just after attacker jumps ___
2. Penetrate into opponent's court ___
3. Jump simultaneously with other blocker ___
4. Withdraw hands ___
5. Return to floor ___
6. Land on two feet ___

Follow-Through

1. Bend knees to cushion landing ___
2. Turn away from net ___
3. Look for the ball ___
4. Return to original position ___
5. Prepare for next play ___

BLOCKING SUCCESS STOPPERS

Mistakes in blocking can be grouped in two categories—errors in technique and errors in timing. Errors in timing usually result in players missing the block completely. Errors in technique often result in the ball being deflected in such a manner that it is difficult for the backcourt defensive players to react.

ERROR	CORRECTION
1. You, the blocker, jump before the attack is complete.	1. Watch the opposing setter until you know where the set will be placed; then watch the attacker until the attacker's hand and the ball are both in view.
2. You return to the floor while the attacker is contacting the ball.	2. Wait to jump until just after the attacker jumps.
3. The fingers of your hands are closed.	3. Spread the fingers of your hands wide so that your thumbs are pointing at the ceiling.
4. You land with straight legs.	4. You must bend your knees upon landing for cushioning.
5. You line up body-to-body with the attacker.	5. Line up one-half body width on the attacker's hitting side.
6. The ball contacts your hands and remains on your side of the net.	6. You must square your shoulders to the net before jumping.
Multiple Block	
1. As the joining blocker, you move into the teammate setting the block.	1. You should focus on the player setting the block, not on the ball.
2. As the joining blocker, you reach toward the attacker's hand.	2. As the joining blocker, you are protecting the angle only and should not reach for the ball.

BLOCKING

DRILLS

1. Toss to Block

In this drill you practice blocking a thrown ball. It allows you to learn how to reach over the net (penetrate) into your opponent's court and direct the ball downward.

Have a partner be a tosser on one side of the net; you be a blocker on the opposite side. The tosser, using a two-handed overhead throw, jumps and throws the ball over the net in a downward motion. Jump and attempt to block the ball before it penetrates the net. The blocked ball should land within the boundaries of the opposite court.

Success Goal = 6 out of 10 good blocks ___

✔**Success Check**
- No arm swing ___
- Fingers spread wide, thumbs point to ceiling ___
- Penetrate net with hands ___
- Bend knees to cushion landing ___

To Increase Difficulty
- Vary distance of throw from the net.
- Throw the ball slightly to the left or to the right.

To Decrease Difficulty
- Blocker stands on a chair.

2. Blind Blocking

This drill forces the blocker to focus on the attacker rather than the ball. This is difficult for beginners to learn.

For this drill you need a group of three—the blocker (yourself) and a tosser on one side of the net, and a spiker on the opposite side of the net. From a position behind you, the tosser throws the ball over the net, high and relatively close to the net. The attacker jumps and spikes the ball, aiming at you, the blocker. Jump and attempt to block the ball back at the attacker; it should land inbounds.

Success Goal = 4 good blocks out of 10 attempts ___

✔**Success Check**
- Line up on attacker's hitting side ___
- Jump after attacker jumps ___
- Penetrate over net ___
- Bend knees to cushion landing ___

To Increase Difficulty
- Tosser moves the toss around, making the blocker adjust.
- Tosser throws lower.

To Decrease Difficulty
- Tosser tosses close to the net.
- Toss to the same spot every time.
- Blocker stands on a chair.

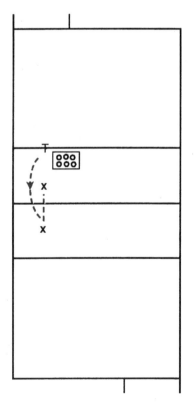

3. Double Blocking

In this drill the middle blocker practices joining the outside blocker. The middle blocker must recognize that it's the outside blocker's responsibility to set the block and take the ball. The middle blocker is responsible for the angle.

Have a group of four take the roles of a tosser and an attacker on one side of the net, and two blockers on the opposite side. One blocker should be near the middle of the court, the other near the sideline.

The tosser tosses the ball high and outside to the attacker, who is near the sideline at the attack line. The attacker approaches and spikes the ball over the net. The middle blocker joins the outside blocker, who has set the block, to form a double block.

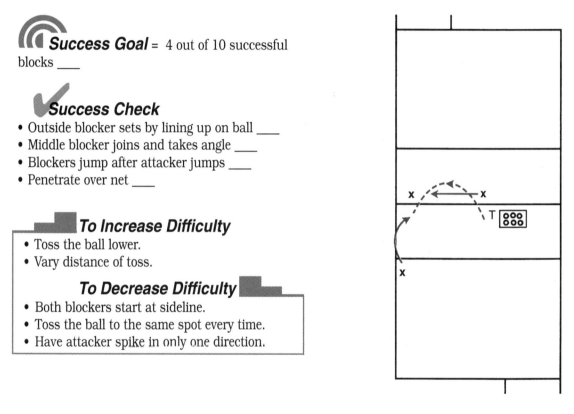

Success Goal = 4 out of 10 successful blocks ___

Success Check
• Outside blocker sets by lining up on ball ___
• Middle blocker joins and takes angle ___
• Blockers jump after attacker jumps ___
• Penetrate over net ___

To Increase Difficulty
• Toss the ball lower.
• Vary distance of toss.

To Decrease Difficulty
• Both blockers start at sideline.
• Toss the ball to the same spot every time.
• Have attacker spike in only one direction.

4. Endurance Blocking

In this drill the blockers practice blocking and then immediately moving off the net to the attack line, getting ready for a transition attack. If the block is successful in putting the ball down, there will be no transition play and the drill begins again. Transition occurs only when there is no block or when the blockers direct the ball upward.

This drill requires a group of eight players—two combination blocker-hitters, one setter, and one overhead passer on each side of the net. Passers should have a supply of balls (at least 10) readily available. On one side of the net, team A's two hitters begin on the attack line (see diagram), and the setter begins at the net. On the opposite side of the net, team B's two blockers are in a ready position, and the setter is in the right back position. Both passers are in their respective backcourt areas.

The passer on the hitter's side (team A) begins the drill by passing the ball high to the setter, who sets either hitter. The blockers on team B react with a single block if it is a quick set, or a double block if it is a high outside set or back set. The blocked ball should land in the attackers' court; the attackers don't need to return it.

The team B passer immediately overhead passes another ball high to the penetrating setter, who sets one of the team B hitters (in the role of blocker just seconds before). The team A blockers (earlier, hitters) react to the attack with a good block. The drill continues indefinitely, the hitters and blockers constantly changing roles like this.

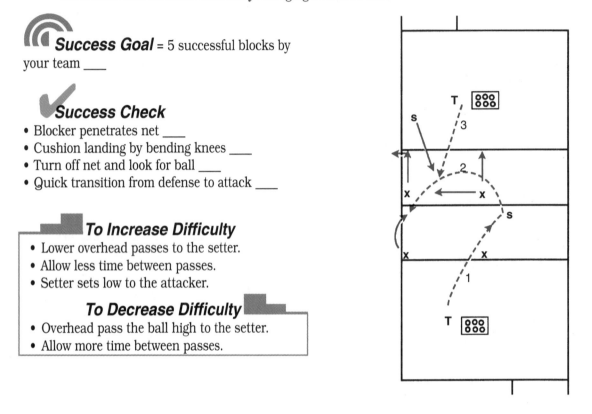

 **Success Goal** = 5 successful blocks by your team ___

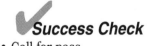 **Success Check**
- Blocker penetrates net ___
- Cushion landing by bending knees ___
- Turn off net and look for ball ___
- Quick transition from defense to attack ___

To Increase Difficulty
- Lower overhead passes to the setter.
- Allow less time between passes.
- Setter sets low to the attacker.

To Decrease Difficulty
- Overhead pass the ball high to the setter.
- Allow more time between passes.

5. Combining Six Skills

The next two drills allow you to practice receiving your opponent's spike and digging it well enough to allow for a possible offense on transition.

In a group of six, have a server, a blocker, and a digger on one side of the net; and a passer, a setter, and an attacker on the other side. The server serves an underhand serve to the right back of the court. The passer forearm passes the ball to the setter, who sets high and outside to the attacker. The attacker spikes the ball over the net on the diagonal toward the digger. The blocker and the digger each attempt to play the ball. The blocker tries to keep the ball on the opponent's side. If this fails, the digger should place the ball high to the center of the digger's side of the court.

 **Success Goal** =
10 out of 12 good serves ___
8 out of 10 successful forearm pass-set-spike combinations ___
5 out of 10 successful blocks or digs ___

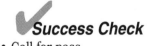 **Success Check**
- Call for pass ___
- Pass high to setter ___
- Block one-half body width to hitting side ___

To Increase Difficulty

- Vary the serves.
- Serve to any location on the court.
- Blocker varies positioning, taking the line or taking the angle.

To Decrease Difficulty

- Toss instead of serve the ball over the net.
- Serve directly at the receiver.
- The blocker takes the line.

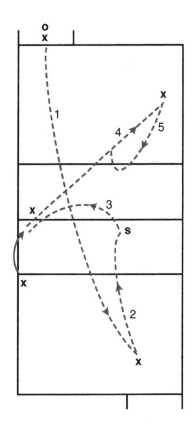

6. Combining Six Skills, Back Set

This is the same as the previous drill, with the exception that the serve goes to the left back of the court, the setter back sets, and the attacker hits from the right sideline on the diagonal.

Success Goal =

10 out of 12 good serves ___
8 out of 10 successful forearm pass-set-spike
  combinations ___
5 out of 10 successful blocks or digs ___

Success Check

- Call for pass ___
- Pass high to setter ___
- Attacker calls for set ___
- Block one-half body width to hitting side ___

To Increase Difficulty

- Vary the serves.
- Serve to any location on the court.
- Blocker varies positioning, taking the line or taking the angle.

To Decrease Difficulty

- Toss instead of serve the ball over the net.
- Toss or serve directly at the receiver.
- The blocker takes the line.

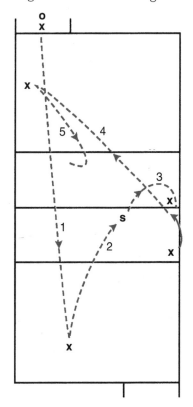

7. Five-Player Reception

This drill allows you to practice six on six. It simulates actual game play, but you continue serving from the same position and side for a given number of serves. The ball is not played out in transition.

Six players set up on each side of the court. The server on one side serves underhand. The receiving team—in the W-formation—attempts a pass-set-spike combination, the set going alternately to the left forward and right forward and the spike going on the diagonal. The serving team attempts to block with a double block. Any ball not successfully blocked should be dug high to the center of the digger's side.

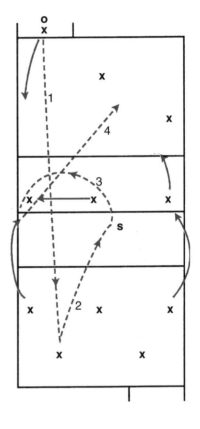

Success Goal =
10 out of 12 good serves ___
8 out of 10 accurate forearm pass-set-spike
   combinations ___
5 out of 10 successful blocks or digs ___

Success Check
• Call for serve early ___
• Open up to (turn and face) receiver ___
• Set ball high to outside of court ___
• Outside blocker sets block, middle blocker
   joins ___

To Increase Difficulty
• Vary the serve's force and direction.
• Vary the set direction, to the left front and right
   front.
• Vary the height of the set.

To Decrease Difficulty
• Toss rather than serve the ball.
• Serve directly at the receiver.
• Indicate which attacker will receive the set.

8. Six-Player Modified Game

This drill simulates regular game play with the exception that rotation is delayed until 10 serves have been made to allow players to learn one position well before rotating. The scoring system encourages teams to work toward the three-hit combination.

Six players set up on each side of the court. The player in each center front position is the team's setter. The W-formation is used for serve reception. Each team makes 5 consecutive serves. After 10 serves, the players on both teams rotate one position clockwise.

The ball is rallied as in a regular volleyball game. The team that wins the rally scores a point. When a team successfully completes a pass-set-spike combination, it scores an additional point. For a bad serve, subtract a point from the team's score.

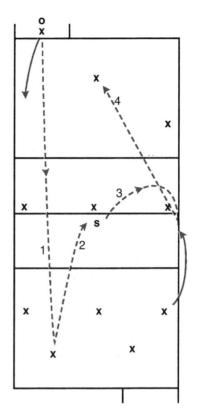

Success Goal = be the team earning the greater number of points after six rotations (60 total serves) ___

Success Check
- Call for the serve early ___
- Open up to receiver ___
- Set ball high to outside of court ___
- Outside blocker sets block; middle blocker joins ___

To Increase Difficulty
- Vary the serve's force and direction.
- Vary the set direction.
- Vary the height of the set.
- Subtract 2 points for a bad serve.

To Decrease Difficulty
- Toss rather than serve the ball.
- Serve directly at the receiver.
- Indicate which attacker will receive the set.
- Add 3 points for every successful three-hit combination.

BLOCKING SUCCESS SUMMARY

As with the dig, successful blocking is based on your ability to read your opponent's attack. The biggest error committed by a beginner is following the trajectory of the ball rather than concentrating on the attacker for whom he or she is responsible. An indication that you may be doing this is if you often attempt to block even when the attacker does not complete the attack. Unnecessarily blocking and touching the net is an extremely costly error.

Have another skilled player or volleyball person evaluate your blocking form with the Keys to Success checklist in Figures 7.1 and 7.2.

STEP 8

SIMPLE OFFENSE: ATTACKING WITH TWO FRONT ROW PLAYERS

The ball is served into your court by the opponent. Three players call for the ball and collide as they all attempt to play it. They all look at each other in frustration, each feeling that it was her ball to play! It is essential to organize your play so that a different formation is used for each situation that occurs during a rally. The organization of your court movement into different formations is referred to as offense or defense.

There are two categories of offenses in volleyball—simple and multiple. Generally, the simple offenses are used at beginning levels of play, while the multiple offenses are employed by higher skilled teams. Simple offenses, including the 4-2 and International 4-2, will be discussed in this step.

Simple Offenses

Once you master the basic skills and begin to compete in actual game situations, you should learn and use various offensive and defensive strategies. This enhances communication between you and the other players, and helps maintain organized patterns of play. The first strategy that you should learn is the 4-2 offense, considered to be the easiest offense to execute.

Offensive alignments are usually titled numerically; the first number refers to the number of players who serve primarily as attackers and the second number refers to the number of players who serve primarily as setters. Therefore, in the 4-2 offense, four players are attackers and two players are setters.

The International 4-2 offense is similar to the regular 4-2 offense in that four players function primarily as attackers and two players are primarily setters. The difference is the position the setter takes at the net. In the regular 4-2, the setter assumes the center front position. In the International 4-2, the setter assumes the right front position. When covering the International 4-2, only the implications of this difference will be discussed.

Why Are the 4-2 and International 4-2 Offenses Important?

The 4-2 offense is usually the first offense a team learns. It is called a *simple offense* because the setter is one of the front row players. Only front row players may spike from in front of the attack line; therefore, if one of these players serves as the setter, the team is limited to only two front line attackers. Many teams do not have more than four highly skilled attackers, so these teams find the 4-2 offense adequate. Teams often select an offensive system which is too complicated for the skill level of their available athletes.

Many teams prefer the International 4-2 over the regular 4-2 because the location of the setter (right forward position) means that both attackers, if right-handed, are hitting on-hand. This implies that the team is attacking from the most powerful position. A disadvantage of the International 4-2 comes when your setter is small in stature, because the setup dictates that the setter blocks the opponent's strong side attacker.

How to Execute the 4-2 and International 4-2 Offenses

When examining each offense, this text discusses three areas: serve reception, covering the attacker, and free ball formation. *Serve reception* is when your team is receiving the serve from the opponents. *Covering the attacker* is the action taken to efficiently cover the court during a spike by your team that may be blocked by the opponents. A *free ball formation* is the position taken by your team to receive a ball coming from your opponent that is neither a serve nor a spike. In the serve reception and free ball situations, your team is receiving the ball and is in transition from defense to offense.

Over the years, many serve reception patterns have been introduced. The current thought in this area is that the fewer people assigned to receive the serve, the better the result. Many teams therefore employ two-person, three-person, or four-person serve reception formations. The traditional W-formation remains the most prevalent serve reception pattern at the beginning levels of play. For purposes of this book, we will concentrate on the W-formation because when it is employed, all players have the opportunity to experience serve reception.

In any serve reception formation, the setter does not want to receive the serve under any circumstances. The setter, therefore, assumes a position either near the net or behind another player (hides).

Until the ball is actually contacted on the serve, all players on *both* teams must be aligned on the court in their correct rotational positions. *Rotational positions* are the positions that players of both teams must be in during the serve. These positions are indicated on the lineup submitted by the coach before the game. *Playing positions* are the positions assumed by players on the court immediately after the serve is executed. Players can assume any position on the court at that time, with the exception that only the forwards may attack or block from in front of the attack line.

Because players are allowed to play any position on the court after the serve is initiated, specialization has become very popular. When a team employs specialization, each player basically plays two positions: one while in the front line and one while in the back line. Because teams rotate each time they gain a side out, players would need to master six different positions on the court if teams did not specialize. Obviously, specialization facilitates the learning process. When the W-formation for serve reception is diagramed, the players are indicated according to their rotational positions and their functions—for example, attacker or setter—but not

according to their specialization.

The International 4-2 is similar to the regular 4-2; therefore, your team should find it easy to move from one to the other. Because there are attackers in the left forward and center forward positions, your team can become accustomed to using a middle attack. This prepares you for advancing to a multiple offense.

Serve Reception

In the 4-2 offense, a setter always sets from the middle of the court close to the net. Two players serve as setters. In the lineup, the setters should be in opposition to one another; that is, left forward and right back, center forward and center back, or right forward and left back. Initially the setters are positioned in the center forward and center back positions. The setter who is the center forward is responsible for the setting duties until rotating into the right back position. At that time, the second setter rotates into the left forward position and assumes the active role of setting. The W-formation is diagramed here for three rotations (see Diagrams 8.1, 8.2, and 8.3). The remaining three rotations repeat the patterns demonstrated in the three diagramed, with the exception that the players will be in opposing positions.

Note in the diagrams that the setter always "hides" at the net and begins in the correct rotational position. As soon as the serve is contacted, the setter moves to the center front of the court, gaining two

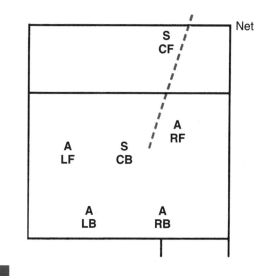

Diagram 8.1 W-formation, serve reception, 4-2 offense, setter in the CF position.

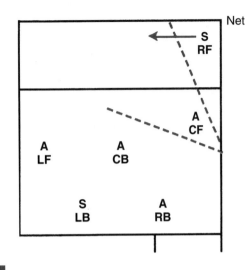

Diagram 8.2 W-formation, serve reception, 4-2 offense, setter in the RF position.

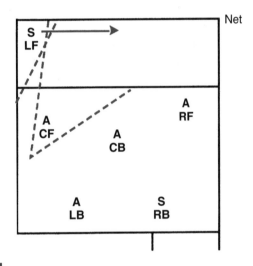

Diagram 8.3 W-formation, serve reception, 4-2 offense, setter in the LF position.

options for attack—a front set or a back set. The setter always faces the left sideline, having the right foot forward (the foot closer to the net). The setter remains in this position directing the attack until the next serve. When the team is comprised of all right-handed players, the left side of the court is the strong side because the left forward is attacking on-hand.

In Diagram 8.1, the setter is the center forward and no switch is necessary. In Diagrams 8.2 and 8.3, the setter must switch from an outside position to the center of the court. In each of these last two cases, the center forward attacker is in position on

the same side of the court as the setter and is preparing to become an outside attacker.

Teams must be aware of the potential for overlap in these two alignments. Lines are drawn in the diagrams to indicate the problem areas of overlap (Diagrams 8.2 and 8.3). The center back must remain behind the center forward, and the setter must be sure to remain closer to the sideline than the center forward when the ball is served.

To receive serve efficiently, a team must utilize certain guidelines. The back line players always position themselves so that they have a clear view of the server as they look between the front line players. The player receiving serve must call for the ball before it crosses the plane of the net. All players must turn and face the player who has called for the ball; this action is referred to as *opening up* to the ball. No players should receive any serve that is chest high or above; the front row players should allow the back row players to receive this serve, and the back row players should allow this serve to go out.

The setter and center back players should signal their teammates if a serve is short. The right and left back players function as a team, helping each other call "out" on any ball that is long; one player calls for the ball, and the second watches and decides whether to call it out. The left forward with the left back, and the right forward with the right back, act as teams to call the left sideline and the right sideline. When any player calls for the ball, the matched player decides whether the serve is good or out-of-bounds. Any "watcher" must call "out" as soon as possible, so that the receiver does not attempt to play the ball. The player who calls for a ball should move to the best position to receive it. No player who calls for a ball should call it out unless on the line when making the call.

Serve reception is a total team effort and requires concentration and communication. If only one member of the team does not assume the responsibility given, the entire team may fail.

Diagram 8.4 indicates the areas of responsibility for each of the five players during serve reception. Serve reception formation for the International 4-2 is close to the W-formation for the regular 4-2. The only differences are based upon the location of the setter. The setters begin in the right forward and left back positions. In the initial W-formation, no switch by the setter is necessary. It is the right back who moves toward the attack line and appears to be a

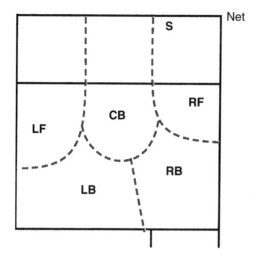

Diagram 8.4 Areas of serve-reception responsibility for all players when using the W-formation.

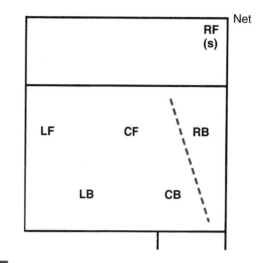

Diagram 8.5a Serve reception when setter is RF, using the International 4-2.

Summary of Player Responsibilities for Successful Serve Reception

All Players

- decide who will receive the ball as soon as possible after contact by the server,
- call for the ball before it crosses the plane of the net,
- open up to the player playing the ball, and
- help call the ball out-of-bounds for other players.

Front Row Players

- allow balls that are higher than chest level to be played by back row players,
- do not move more than one step back to play the ball,
- call the ball out on the sideline for the back row player on the same side of the court, and
- are ready to move forward quickly on short serves.

Back Row Players

- allow a ball that is at chest height or higher to go out-of-bounds,
- call the ball out on the sideline for the front row player on the same side of the court,
- are more aggressive from the left back position in receiving when the ball is between the left and right backs,
- call the ball out over the end line for the other back, and
- always position themselves between the front row players.

Setters

- never receive serve,
- call short serves,
- call for the pass and extend the hand closer to the net high as a target for the passer, and
- face the left sideline with the right foot forward in the stride position.

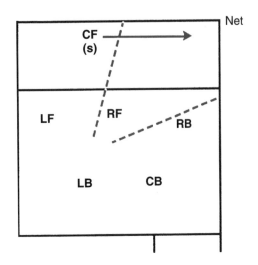

Diagram 8.5b Serve reception when setter is CF, using the International 4-2.

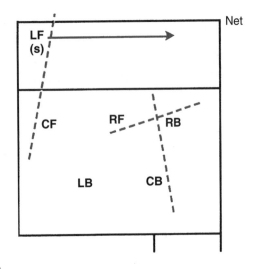

Diagram 8.5c Serve reception when setter is LF, using the International 4-2.

forward line player as illustrated in Diagram 8.5a. Diagrams 8.5b and c illustrate serve reception positioning when the setter is the center forward and the left forward. Notice that the players always align themselves so that the two attacking forwards receive in the left court area and the setter moves to the right forward position.

Covering the Attacker

Once your team has received the serve and has passed to the setter, you attempt to complete an offensive attack. There are five possible outcomes of every attack. In three of these outcomes, the ball

becomes dead and play is completed. The results that end in a dead ball are (a) the attacker spikes the ball to the floor for a point, (b) the attacker spikes the ball out-of-bounds or makes an error, or (c) the blocker blocks the ball out-of-bounds or makes an error.

In the fourth and fifth attack outcomes, the ball remains in play. Either the defensive team digs the ball and prepares for a counterattack, or the blocker(s) successfully blocks the ball and it remains on your side of the court. If the opposing block is successful, the ball remains in play, falling quickly to the floor in an area directly behind the attacker. Therefore, this is the critical area for your team to cover.

In the 3-2 coverage, three of your players make a semicircle behind the attacker, while the remaining two players position themselves in the spaces between them (see Diagram 8.6a and b). The person closest to the sideline is the back row player on the same side of the court as the attacker. The person in the middle of the three is *always* the center back. The player closest to the net is always the setter, who sets the attacker and follows the set by moving to the coverage position. These three players must be in a low defensive position to have as much time as possible to react to the ball. They should be looking at the blocker's hands when the ball is contacted by your spiker.

The two offensive players toward the sideline opposite the attacker's side shift toward the attack side and align themselves in the spaces between the three-

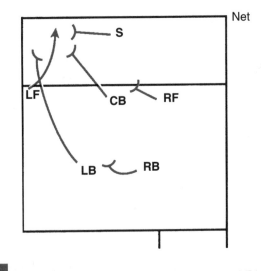

Diagram 8.6a Spike coverage when your LF is spiking.

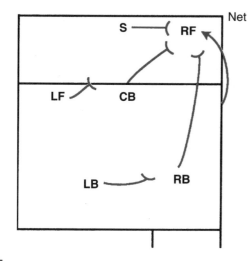

Diagram 8.6b Spike coverage when your RF is spiking.

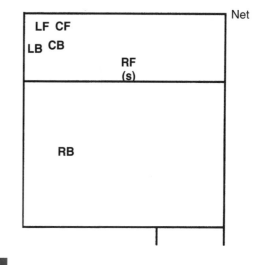

Diagram 8.7a Spike coverage, LF spiking, International 4-2.

player semicircle. Diagram 8.6a illustrates the 3-2 coverage when your left forward is attacking; Diagram 8.6b illustrates the 3-2 coverage when your right forward is attacking.

If the ball goes by or is deflected by the block and is dug by the defense, your team must quickly assume the base defensive formation. This formation will be covered during the discussion of defense.

In the International 4-2, the coverage of the attacker is similar to that used in the regular 4-2. The same 3-2 formation is used: three people form a semicircle around the attacker, and the remaining two players shift and fill the spaces between those three. The differences are in which players assume which positions in the formation and that the two attackers are now coming from the center forward and left forward positions rather than the left forward and right forward positions. Refer to Diagrams 8.7a and 8.7b for proper coverage in the International 4-2. When the attacker is the left forward, the left back, center back, and right back are in the same positions and have the same responsibilities as in the regular 4-2. The center forward and right forward are also in the same positions, but the center forward is now an attacker, and the right forward the setter; this is reversed from the alignment in the regular 4-2. In the coverage for an attack by the center forward, the left forward, center back, and setter (right forward) form the semicircle around the attacker, while the left back and the right back align themselves in the spaces between those three players.

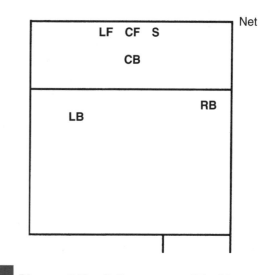

Diagram 8.7b Spike coverage, CF spiking, International 4-2.

Free Ball

Any time the opposing team is playing the ball and attempting to set its attack, your team's blockers are at the net anticipating their next action to be a block. When it becomes obvious that the opposing team does not have enough control to complete their attack, your team must prepare to receive a free ball. Lack of control is often indicated when the first pass does not go toward the net, when a player other than the setter must handle the second ball, when the set is made to a distance of more than 10 feet off the net, or when the attacker is out of position.

The free ball formation is very similar to the W-formation. The only difference is that the setter is already in position at the center front of the court. The setter usually calls "free" to communicate with the team that no block is necessary. Your team should immediately move to free ball formation. The setter remains at the net, the two attackers move straight back to the attack line, and the center back moves close to the attack line at the center of the court. The remaining two backs fill in the spaces between the forwards.

The attackers' first priority is to receive the ball; their second priority is to prepare to attack. As soon as the two attackers are sure that they will not have to receive the free ball, they move to the sidelines of the court and prepare to receive the set. It is critical that the attackers do not "wing out" like this (see Diagram 8.8) until they are positive that the free ball will be passed by a teammate. The number 1 on the diagram indicates the direction of the attackers' first movement straight back to the attack line. The number 2 on the diagram is the wing out, or second movement, by the attacker to a position outside the sidelines in preparation for the attack. Once the free ball is received, your team sets its own attack and proceeds with appropriate coverage.

In the International 4-2, the free ball formation is the same W used in the regular 4-2. The difference is that the setter is the right forward. This implies that the two attackers moving off the net are now in the left forward and center forward positions, the setter remains at the net, the right back must move forward into what appears to be a front line position, and the center back must move right and fill the right point of the W. Diagram 8.9 illustrates the movement of the players from base defense to free ball position in the International 4-2.

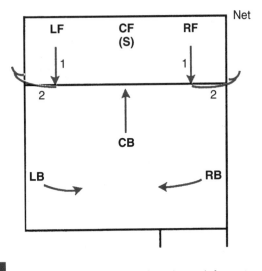

Diagram 8.8   Movement from base defense to free ball.

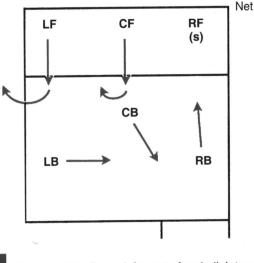

Diagram 8.9   Base defense to free ball, International 4-2.

SIMPLE OFFENSE SUCCESS STOPPERS

Errors in the execution of the 4-2 offense can be categorized into three main areas: (a) not assuming the position indicated by the play situation; (b) moving toward the correct position, but not arriving at that spot soon enough; and (c) assuming the correct position, but executing poorly. Errors in all three offensive formations—serve reception, covering the attacker, and free ball—can be included in the first category above. Errors in covering the attacker and free ball are more frequently found in the second category. Serve reception errors are most commonly found in category three.

Errors made when using the International 4-2 are similar to those indicated for the regular 4-2. The main difference is in the location and movement of the setter and the right back player. Often it is the failure of the right back to adjust to the setter's location that causes errors.

ERROR	CORRECTION
1. The setter receives the serve.	1. Setter should hide at net and not receive the serve under any circumstances.
2. A free ball falls between a front row player and a back row player.	2. The two forwards must move quickly off the net to the attack line and assume a ready position prior to the opponent making contact with the ball.
3. The ball rebounds off the opponent's block and falls to the floor on the attacker's side.	3. Three players must assume a coverage position around the attacker.
4. A player in the W-formation gets hit on the back by a passed ball.	4. All players must open up to the receiver by turning and facing that player.
5. The serve falls to the court between two players.	5. Receivers must call for the serve prior to the ball's crossing the net.
6. The ball rebounds off the block and falls to the court between the coverage and the sideline.	6. The player covering the line should have the outside foot on the sideline and should not play a ball that rebounds off the block beyond the sideline side of the body.
7. The attacker prevents the coverage from playing the ball.	7. The attacker should not play a ball that rebounds off the block unless it stays between the attacker and the net.

Errors Specific to International 4-2

8. A free ball falls to the court in the right forward position.	8. The setter is the right forward and remains at the net; therefore, the right back must adjust and cover this area of the court.
9. The setter attempts to back set.	9. The two eligible attackers are in the center forward and left forward positions; there is no right forward attacker to whom to back set.

SIMPLE OFFENSE

DRILLS

1. Wing Out

In this drill you practice free ball movement as an attacker. Movement should be in two phases—straight back to the attack line, then, after receiving the ball, winging out to get ready for your approach.

Place a chair at the attack line at the left sideline (see Diagram a, next page). You need two partners for this drill. One is a setter, positioned at the net in the middle of the court. You are a left forward in blocking position on the same side of the court as the chair. Your other partner is a tosser on the opposite side of the net.

The tosser yells "free" and tosses the ball high and easy to the attack line. You, the left forward, move straight back to the attack line, overhead pass the ball to the setter, wing out around the chair, and approach to complete the attack. The setter sets a high outside set. Repeat this drill on the right side of the court (Diagram b, below). The same drill can be used for the International 4-2 with you as a center forward. When practicing this drill for the International 4-2, the setter should be positioned closer to the right sideline (Diagram c, below).

Success Goal =

8 out of 10 successful attacks from the left forward position ___

7 out of 10 successful attacks from the right forward position ___

7 out of 10 successful attacks from the center forward position ___

Success Check

• Move to attack line quickly ___
• Set position before passing ___
• Pass ball high and wing out ___
• Begin approach when set reaches highest point ___

To Increase Difficulty

• Place the chair farther from the net.
• Toss the ball lower.
• Toss the ball to various locations.
• Setter makes lower sets.

To Decrease Difficulty

• Place chair closer to the net.
• Toss the ball at only one height.
• Toss to the same spot every time.
• Setter sets the ball high.

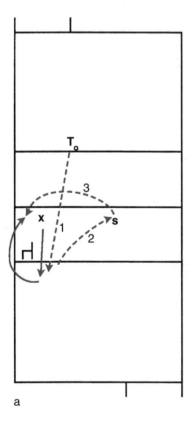

a

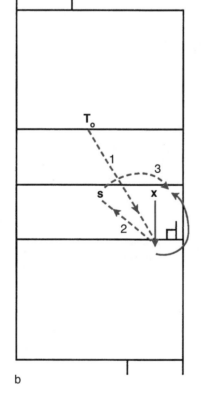

b

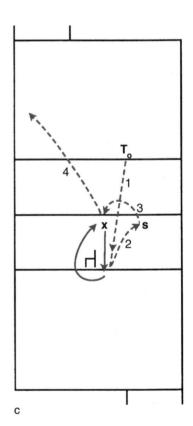

c

2. Serve Reception

In this drill you practice receiving serve as a team, setting up your attack, and covering your attacker. Make sure that you practice all the rules of good serve reception—calling for the ball, calling the ball out and short, playing balls only at the correct height, etc.

A team of six lines up on one side of the court (see Diagram a, below). A server on the opposite side of the court serves the ball underhand to the receiving team. The team goes into a W-formation with the setter in the center forward position. The team receives the serve, executes an attack either forward or back, and covers the attacker correctly.

The team receives five good serves, then rotates one position. Continue this drill until all players have rotated around to the original starting positions. This drill can also be used for the International 4-2 (see Diagram b, below).

Success Goal = 24 out of 30 successful attacks with the correct coverage ____

Success Check
- Call loudly for ball ____
- Pass high to setter ____
- Nonreceivers open up ____
- Players be set low in cover positions before contact by attacker ____

To Increase Difficulty
- Vary the serves.
- Serve the ball anywhere on the court.
- Setter sets either front or back.

To Decrease Difficulty
- Serve to a designated person.
- Decide in advance who will spike.

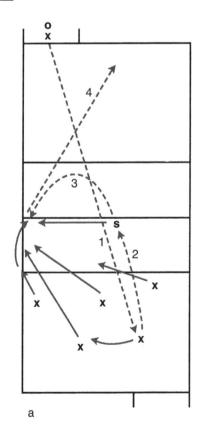

a

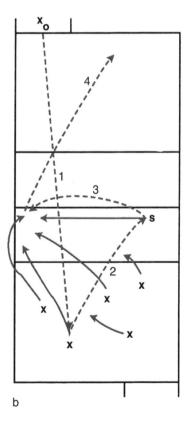

b

3. Free Ball

In this drill you practice receiving a free ball as a team. The setter should repeat the "free" signal of the tosser. The team covers the attacker every time.

A team of six lines up on one side of the court, with the three forwards at the net in blocking position (see Diagram a, below). The center back is in the center of the court, and the left and right backs are on their respective sidelines 20 feet from the net. A tosser is on the opposite side of the net.

The tosser yells "free," delays for a couple of seconds, then tosses the ball over the net high and easy. The team of six quickly moves into the W-formation. They receive the ball, set an attack, and cover the attacker.

The team receives five balls, then rotates one position. Continue this drill until the players have rotated to their original starting positions. This drill can be adapted to suit the International 4-2 formation (see Diagram b, below).

Success Goal = 24 out of 30 successful attacks with the proper coverage ___

Success Check
• Move to attack line quickly ___
• Set position before playing ball ___
• Square shoulders in direction of pass ___
• Low position on coverage ___

To Increase Difficulty
• Toss to various heights and locations.
• Toss quicker after yelling "free."

To Decrease Difficulty
• Start in free ball position.
• Toss to a consistent height.
• Toss to designated receivers.

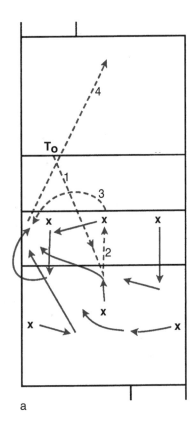

a

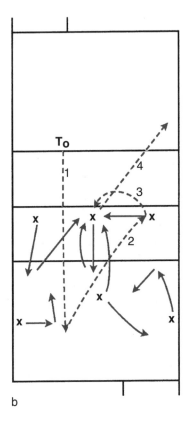

b

4. Cover and Dig

This drill allows the covering team to react and play a blocked ball and attempt an attack in transition, making sure to cover the second attack. As long as the block is successful, the drill will continue.

A team of six stands on one side of the court in the same starting positions as in the free ball drill (see Diagram a, below). Two blockers stand on a box on the right side of the court on the opposite side of the net.

A tosser, on the same court as the blockers, yells "free" and throws a high ball over the net. The team receives the free ball, sets the attack to their left forward, and covers. The blockers block the ball. The attacking coverage attempts to set up with a successful dig to initiate a second attack. The drill can be varied by having the second attack come from the right forward. In this case, the drill would end after two attacks.

The team receives five tosses, then rotates one position. Continue the drill until players have returned to their original positions. Diagram b, below, shows how to adapt this drill for the International 4-2.

Success Goal = 18 out of 30 successful digs off the opposing block ____

Success Check
• Cover in a low position ____
• Dig ball high ____
• Cover second attack ____

To Increase Difficulty
• Vary the height and direction of the tosses.
• Shorten the time between calling "free" and tossing.

To Decrease Difficulty
• Toss high, easy, and directly at the receiver.
• Lengthen the time between calling "free" and tossing.
• The setter sets high.
• The attacker hits the ball directly into the blockers' hands.

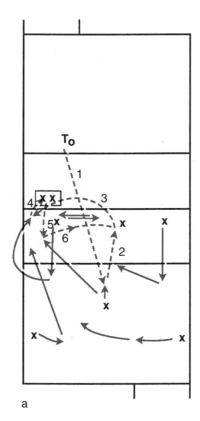

a

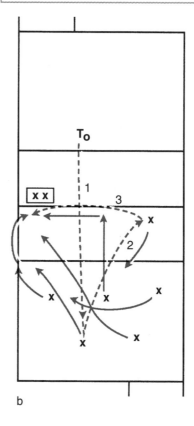

b

5. Serve and Free Ball

In this drill you practice receiving serve, setting up your attack, covering your attacker, and moving into a blocking ready position. Next you receive a free ball and repeat the same action.

Have a team of six on one side of the net, and a tosser and a server each with a ball on the opposite side. The server serves. The receiving team, positioned in the W-formation, receives serve, sets the attack, and covers (see Diagram a, below).

Then the team immediately assumes starting positions as in the free ball drill (see Diagram b, below). The opposing tosser calls "free" and tosses a ball high over the net. The receiving team passes the free ball, sets an attack, and covers. Play continues with another serve and attack immediately followed by another free ball.

The team receives five good serves, then rotates one position. The drill continues until all players return to their starting positions. See Diagrams c and d, next page, to adapt this drill for the International 4-2 formation.

Success Goal =
24 out of 30 successful attacks off serve
   receptions ___
24 out of 30 successful attacks off free balls ___

Success Check
- Quick movement off net ___
- Set in coverage positions before attacker contacts ball ___
- Call ball as soon as possible ___

To Increase Difficulty
- Use any method of serving.
- Serve the seams between potential receivers.
- Vary the free ball toss in height and force.
- Shorten the time between yelling "free" and tossing the ball.

To Decrease Difficulty
- Serve underhand.
- Serve directly to the receiver.
- Wait longer between yelling "free" and tossing the ball.

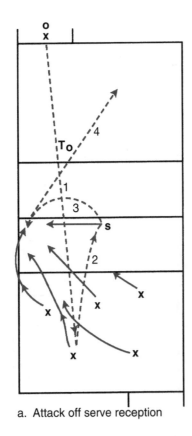

a. Attack off serve reception

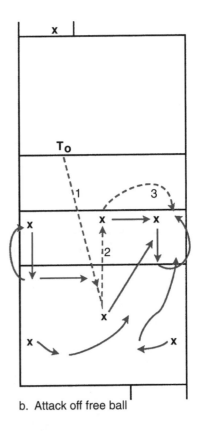

b. Attack off free ball

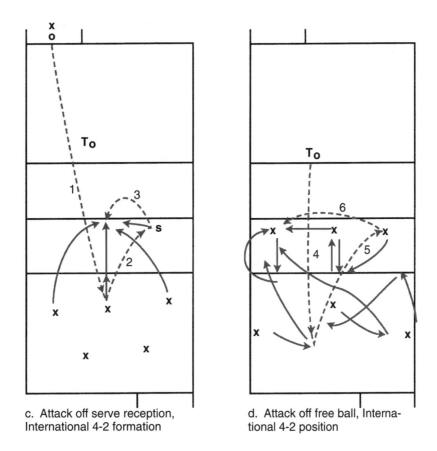

c. Attack off serve reception,
International 4-2 formation

d. Attack off free ball, International 4-2 position

SIMPLE OFFENSE SUCCESS SUMMARY

To be successful as a team, all players need to understand the complexities of each position that they will have to play. They also need to know and understand the responsibilities of their teammates. In competition, you must be organized in your approach. This organization is accomplished by employing situational formations in which all players understand their responsibilities. The simple offenses give teams an opportunity to work on player positioning in the least complex manner.

Have a skilled observer refer to the diagrams of each formation for serve reception, free ball, and coverage of the attacker (Diagrams 8.1-8.9) for the offensive system you have selected (the 4-2 or the International 4-2) to determine if your team is correctly moving into the appropriate positions.

STEP 9

2-1-3 DEFENSE: TRANSITIONING TO ATTACK

Due to a bad forearm pass on serve reception, your team is unable to set up for a spike and must send a free ball to the opponent. The opponent receives the free ball and immediately sets to its best attacker who jumps into the air ready for the kill. You find yourself standing in the middle of the court with the ball headed for your face! You succumb to your natural reaction and duck. The ball hits the floor for the kill. You must cover the court by setting up a defense.

There are two major defensive alignments in volleyball. The 2-1-3 (covered in this step) is stronger against a team that uses tips and off-speed spikes, and the 2-4 is more effective against a powerful attacking team. Other defensive systems—strong or counter rotational—have been developed and are generally adaptations of these two basic formations. Three general principles are always in effect regardless of what defensive system you are employing. First, your team must read what your opponent is planning to do. Second, all players must use this information to decide where to best position themselves. Finally, the players must receive the opponent's attack and set their own attack in transition.

When the ball goes over the net to the opposing team, your team should immediately move to the base defensive formation. This formation is used until the type of ball to be returned from the opponent becomes evident; the two possible plays are either a free ball or an attack. The free ball formation was described in Step 8.

When the opposing team executes an attack, the most effective way of defending it is with a block and backcourt coverage. In the 2-1-3 defense, the 2 represents the blockers, the 1 is a player who is positioned behind the block, and the 3 indicates the backcourt players. When using the 2-1-3 defense, the team assumes that the block will protect at least the deep area of the court behind it. The off-blocker and backcourt players must be strategically positioned to cover the remaining court.

Why Is the 2-1-3 Defense Important?

When your opponent is playing the ball, your team wishes to be in the most advantageous position to react quickly when the ball is returned. An attack takes very little time to travel from the hitter's hand to the floor; therefore, you must be in a position such that your primary action is reacting to the ball rather than covering much ground. The base defensive formation places the blockers close to the net, ready to block, and the backcourt players near the areas they will cover behind the block.

The strength of the 2-1-3 defensive formation is that it affords good protection against a team that makes use of many off-speed attacks and tips. The player behind the block is in position to receive these types of attack easily. To be successful in using the 2-1-3, a team must have strong blocking. If the block is weak, a large portion of the court behind the block is vulnerable. Another important aspect of this defense is that each backcourt player is generally responsible for receiving only one type of attack, either a hard-driven spike or a soft attack (off-speed spike or a tip). This makes the backcourt player's role easier.

How to Execute the 2-1-3 Defense

The 2-1-3 defensive formation is usually the first defensive system learned by beginning teams. Because each player has the responsibility of receiving only one type of attack, the roles are clearly defined and easier to execute. This defense is also strong against other beginning teams because at this level the opponents are more likely to use off-speed attacks and tips than hard-driven spikes.

Base

When using the 2-1-3 defense, in the base formation the center back player remains in the middle of the court. The two attackers and the setter stay at the net, anticipating a block. The remaining two defensive players position themselves 20 feet from the net and close to their respective sidelines (see Diagram 9.1).

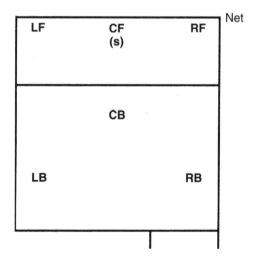

Diagram 9.1 Base defensive formation for the 2-1-3 defense.

The base defensive position is held until a team leader determines whether the team should block or move into a free ball formation. It is extremely important that all players on the team move into the same formation. Even if the team leader errs and calls "free ball" only to have the opposing team attack, the team is still capable of receiving the ball if everyone is in the same formation. If, however, some players block and others move to free ball, some areas on the court will be very vulnerable. Diagram 9.2 shows base defense to free ball formation.

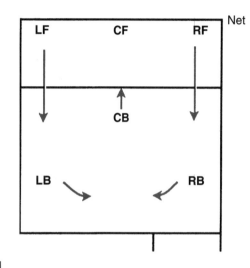

Diagram 9.2 Movement to free ball from base defensive formation.

Block

If the opponent spikes, your team should attempt to block; you must align yourselves behind the block in the most strategic manner. Your team should execute a double block against each spike attempt. The outside blocker decides where to set the block. The blocker should line up half of a body width to the attacker's hitting side. The middle blocker moves to the outside blocker and joins to make a double block. The blocker's hands must be far enough apart to protect as much court area as possible, yet close enough together to prevent the ball from going through the block. The outside blocker's responsibility is the ball. The middle blocker is responsible for the angle.

Once the block is formed, the remaining four players move to positions to cover those parts of the court not protected by the block. Diagram 9.3 indicates the movement of players from the base defensive formation to a blocking formation using the 2-1-3 alignment against an attack from the opposing right forward.

The center forward joins the left forward to form the block. The off-blocker, the right forward, drops

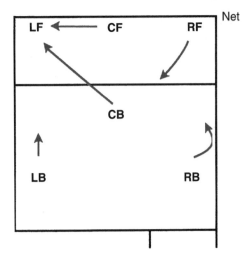

Diagram 9.3 Blocking an attack by the opposing RF, using the 2-1-3 defense.

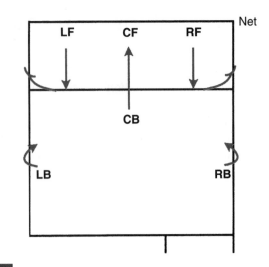

Diagram 9.4 Blocking an attack by the opposing CF, using the 2-1-3 defense.

off the net to the attack line and moves into the court about 10 feet. The off-blocker's responsibilities are handling sharp-angled spikes toward the sideline, tips to the middle of the court close to the net, and "junk" off the net (balls that hit the top of the net, roll, and fall to the court).

The right back is in the part of the court referred to as the *power alley* because any spike that passes the block is likely to go into this area. The right back lines up with his or her back to the sideline and with a line of view to the ball along the center forward's inside shoulder and the attacker's hand. The center back moves to a position immediately behind, and to the middle of, the block in a low defensive posture. The center back's responsibility is any off-speed spike or tip directed over the block, down-the-line, or to the center of the court. The left back is positioned on the sideline 20 feet from the net and has the responsibility to receive any attacks directed down-the-line.

Diagrams 9.4 and 9.5 show the movement of players when defending against an opposing attack from the center forward and left forward, respectively. Note that when the opposing center forward is attacking, the team is using a single blocker and both off-blockers move to the attack line to play defensive roles. This attack is usually a quick attack; the outside blockers find it difficult to have enough time to

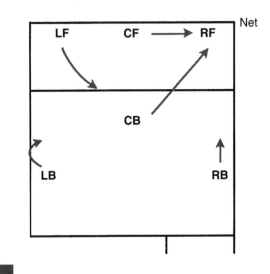

Diagram 9.5 Blocking an attack by the opposing LF, using the 2-1-3 defense.

join the center forward to form a double or a triple block. The responsibilities of each player on defense are similar for all positions, even though the attack is from a different area.

When the ball is directed between two defensive players, both players move laterally toward the ball, with the player closer to the net crossing in front of the deeper player. If all players follow this concept, there should be no collisions between them (see Diagram 9.6).

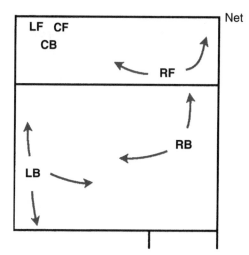

Diagram 9.6 Player movement to dig attacks directed between two players.

Summary for Successful Defense

All Players

- should anticipate play of opponent by attempting to read what the opponent will do, and
- move to the defensive position, set, and be ready to react before the ball is contacted by the attacker.

Front Row Players

- should have hands at shoulder level or higher in starting position,
- should move along the net left and right but, if blocking, never away from the net and back to the net,
- should have no arm swing,
- must penetrate the net with hands on the block, and
- when playing the off-blocker, move to the attack line ready to play defense.

Backcourt Players

- keep low body posture with weight forward on the toes, and
- move through the ball toward the target.

Off-Blocker

- plays tips to the center of the court and close to the net,
- plays junk off the net, and
- plays hard-driven spikes at the sharp angle to the sideline.

Center Back

- plays in a low posture behind the block, ready to receive tips over the block.

Defensive Players on Line

- must play any spike down-the-line.

Power Alley Player

- aligns so that the inside shoulder of the middle blocker, the ball, and the attacker's hand are all in view, and
- receives spikes or off-speeds into the power alley.

2-1-3 DEFENSE SUCCESS STOPPERS

When discussing errors in the execution of the 2-1-3 defense, we are mainly emphasizing the incorrect position of players. In defending an opposing attack, the defensive alignment has to be ready in a set initial position by the time the ball is contacted by the attacker. The ability of players to read the actions of the opponent greatly enhances defensive success. This ability allows players to move efficiently into the correct initial position low and ready.

ERROR	CORRECTION
1. The ball goes through the block.	1. The middle blocker must close the block.
2. The attacker hits successfully down-the-line.	2. The right or left backs must stay on the line when defending deep behind the block.
3. An attacker successfully tips over the block.	3. The center back must move into position behind and close to the block.
4. The ball rebounds off the player in the power alley and continues out-of-bounds.	4. The power alley players—the left back and right back—position themselves with their backs to the sidelines so that the dig is in front of them and stays on the court.
5. The ball goes off the blockers' hands and out-of-bounds.	5. The outside blocker should turn the hand closer to the sideline in toward the court to keep the ball inbounds.

2-1-3 DEFENSE

DRILLS

1. Digging a Tip: Left Forward Attacker

In this drill the center back and the left forward work together to cover the court against a tip by the opposing left forward. As they practice digging the tip, they begin to understand their area of responsibility.

On one side of the net, there is a setter and an attacker in the left forward position. On the opposite side, there are three blockers and a center back.

The attacker tosses the ball to the setter, who sets the ball back to the attacker. The attacker tips the ball over the block, either down-the-line or to the center of the court. The center back covers tips down-the-line, and the off-blocker covers tips to the center of the court.

Success Goal =
on defense, successfully digging 8 of 10 tips ___
on offense, successfully tipping 10 out of 12
    sets ___

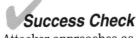**Success Check**
• Attacker approaches as if to spike ___
• Blockers yell "tip" every time ___
• Diggers read attacker to determine tip direction ___
• Defensive player moves quickly to ball and digs it
    high ___

To Increase Difficulty
- Vary the height of the set.
- Attacker occasionally spikes a hard-driven ball.

To Decrease Difficulty
- The attacker does not vary the direction of the tip.

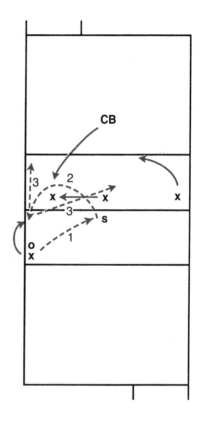

2. Digging a Tip: Right Forward Attacker

In this drill the center back and the right forward work together to cover the court against a tip by the opposing right forward. As they practice digging the tip, they begin to understand their areas of responsibility.

This is the same as the previous drill, except that the attacker is in the right forward position. Another player is needed to toss the ball to the setter, who back sets to the attacker.

Success Goal =
on defense, successfully digging 8 out of 10 tips ___
on offense, successfully tipping 10 out of 12 sets ___

Success Check
- Attacker approaches as if to spike ___
- Blockers yell "tip" every time ___
- Digger reads attacker to determine tip direction ___
- Defensive players move quickly to ball and dig it high ___

To Increase Difficulty
- The setter varies the height of the set.
- The attacker occasionally spikes a hard-driven ball to keep the defensive player honest.

To Decrease Difficulty
- The attacker does not vary the direction of the tip.

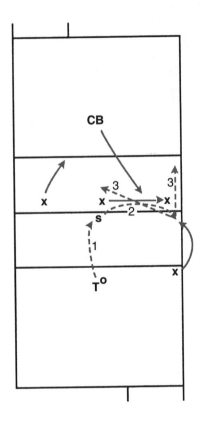

3. Digging Down-the-Line Spikes: Right Back

In this drill the right back practices digging down-the-line spikes. The center forward, setter in the 4-2 offense, practices setting the dig in transition.

On one side of the net, there are three blockers and a right back defending the line. On the opposite side, there are a left forward and a setter.

The attacker tosses the ball to the setter, who sets high and outside. The blockers give the attacker the line (they line up to block only the angle). The attacker spikes the ball down-the-line. The right back digs the ball high to the center of the court, and the center forward sets an attack.

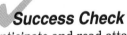 **Success Goal** =

10 out of 12 down-the-line spikes by the attacker ___

6 out of 10 successful digs by the right back ___

4 out of 6 completed attacks on the transition ___

Success Check
- Anticipate and read attack ___
- Move to position ___
- Be low and ready ___
- Dig ball high ___

To Increase Difficulty
- Do not use a block.
- The setter varies the height of the set.

To Decrease Difficulty
- The setter sets the ball a greater distance from the net.
- The blockers attempt to take the line away from the attacker.

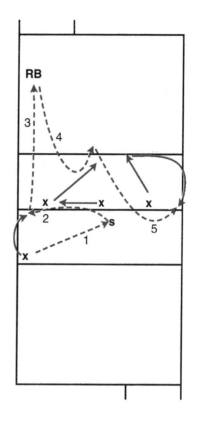

4. Digging Down-the-Line Spikes: Left Back

In this drill, the left back practices digging down-the-line spikes. The center forward, setter in the 4-2 offense, practices back setting to the right forward in transition.

This is the same as the previous drill, with the exception that the attacker is in the right forward position, and the left back digs the spiked balls. Another player should toss the ball to the setter, who back sets to the attacker.

Success Goal =
10 out of 12 down-the-line spikes by the attacker ___
6 out of 10 successful digs by the left back ___
4 out of 6 completed attacks on the transition ___

Success Check
- Anticipate and read attack ___
- Move to position ___
- Be low and ready ___
- Dig ball high ___

To Increase Difficulty
- Do not use a block.
- Vary the height of the set.

To Decrease Difficulty
- Set the ball farther from the net.
- Blockers try to take the line away from the attacker.

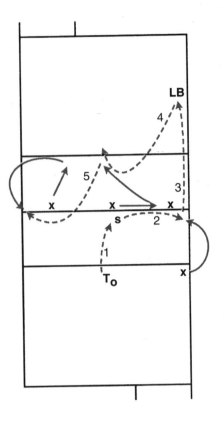

5. Digging Cross-Court: Left Back

In this drill the left forward attacker spikes cross-court. The left back and left forward of the defending team practice digging the cross-court spikes and converting the dig into their own attack in transition. The setter can be either the center forward, as in the 4-2 offense, or the right forward as in the International 4-2.

On one side of the net, there are three blockers and a left back defensive player. On the opposite court, there are a setter and an attacker in the left forward position.

The attacker tosses the ball to the setter, who sets high and outside. The attacker spikes cross-court. The left back or off-blocker digs the ball, and the forwards attempt to complete an attack on transition.

Success Goal =
10 out of 12 successful attacks ___
6 out of 10 successful digs ___
4 out of 6 completed attacks on the transition ___

Success Check
- Backcourt defensive player and off-blocker start with backs to the sideline ___
- Power alley player lines up outside middle blocker's inside shoulder to see attacker and ball ___
- Low position, with weight forward ___
- Once forward movement begins, move through ball ___

To Increase Difficulty
- Set the ball close to the net.
- Vary the height of the set.
- The attacker varies the direction of the cross-court spike.

To Decrease Difficulty
- The setter sets the ball farther off the net.
- The attacker spikes directly at defensive player.

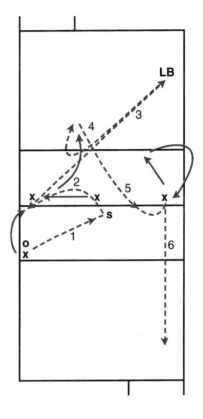

6. Digging Cross-Court: Right Back

In this drill the right forward attacker spikes cross-court. The right forward and the right back on the defending team practice digging cross-court spikes and converting the digs into their own attack in transition. The setter can be either the center forward, as in the 4-2 offense, or the right forward, as in the International 4-2. The center forward would set in either offense if the right forward digs.

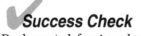

Success Goal =

10 out of 12 successful attacks ___

6 out of 10 successful digs ___

4 out of 6 completed attacks on the transition ___

Success Check

- Backcourt defensive player and off-blocker start with backs to the sideline ___
- Power alley player lines up outside middle blocker's inside shoulder to see attacker and ball ___
- Low position, with weight forward ___
- Once forward movement begins, move through ball ___

 **To Increase Difficulty**

- Set the ball close to the net.
- Vary the height of the set.
- Vary the direction of the cross-court spike.

To Decrease Difficulty

- Set the ball farther off the net.
- Spike directly at the defensive player.

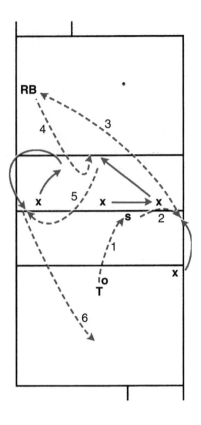

7. Attack and Counterattack

In this drill the toss can be either to the center forward, setter in the 4-2, or to the right forward, setter in an International 4-2 offense. The defending team should react by blocking, using a 2-1-3 if the opponent spikes, or by moving off the net if the result is a free ball. In either case players attempt to attack and cover in transition.

A team of six on one side of the court sets up in base defensive position. A tosser, setter, and two attackers are on the opposite side.

The tosser overhand tosses the ball to the setter, who sets either attacker for a spike. The defending team must block the spike, or receive it and attempt to execute a counterattack. If the attacking players are unable to spike, the defending team should move to a free ball position to receive the third hit over. When the team executes the attack, it must cover the attacker.

The defending team should complete successful counterattacks, then rotate one position. Continue this drill until the players have rotated back to their original positions.

Success Goal =

10 out of 12 successful attacks ___
6 out of 10 successful digs and completed attacks
  on transition ___

Success Check

- Read attack ___
- Assume correct defensive position ___
- Be low and ready ___
- React to ball ___
- Dig high to center of court ___

To Increase Difficulty

- Occasionally toss the ball over the net instead of to the setter.
- Vary the attack as much as possible.
- Direct the attack between two defensive players.
- Setter plays the ball over the net.

To Decrease Difficulty

- Set the ball off the net.
- Select one type and direction of attack and practice it for six attempts.

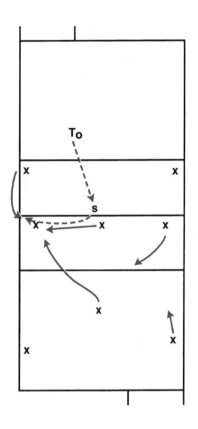

2-1-3 DEFENSE SUCCESS SUMMARY

During a scrimmage a skilled observer should watch your team's movement from the time the ball goes over the net to the opponent until the time your team sets its attack in transition. The first movement should be into base defense. Once in base, you want to see what will develop. If your opponent fails to attack and sends your team a free ball, you quickly move to free ball formation. If your opponent attacks, then you use the 2-1-3 defense. The observer should check to see if your team selects the correct formation and also if all team members are assuming the correct court positions (see Diagrams 9.1 through 9.6).

STEP 10

MULTIPLE OFFENSE: INCREASING OPTIONS ON ATTACK

Y ou have six players on your team who have the ability to spike consistently. Your setters get little chance to demonstrate their attacking ability, however, because you are using a simple offense and they are setting when they are in the front row! You decide that you need more options when you are on attack.

When your team has at least six players who can attack with efficiency, you are ready to employ a multiple offense. If you do not have six players with this ability, it is better to play successfully with a simple offense than to fail with a multiple offense.

The 6-2 and 5-1 offenses are more powerful than either the 4-2 or the International 4-2. The main reason for this is that the setter is a back row player for all six rotations in the 6-2 and for three of the six in the 5-1. When the setter is a back row player, a team can attack from all three forward positions—left, center, and right. The two setters are still opposite each other in the lineup. The setter in the back row performs the setting duties, whereas the setter in the front row is an attacker. All six players attack, and two players have the primary responsibility of setting. The 6-2 is considered a *multiple offense* because the setter penetrates to the net from the back row. This characteristic is indicative of all multiple offenses.

The 5-1 offense is the system that is used most frequently at the international level of play. The 5-1 offense uses only one setter. This means that during three rotations, the setter is in the front row; during the other three rotations, the setter penetrates to the net from the back row. The other five players are attackers, with the player opposite the setter being called the *off-side attacker*.

If your team specializes, it is beneficial to use a left-hander as the off-side attacker because this player would be hitting from the right front position, which is a left-hander's strong side. The setter can become extremely deceptive and effective in attacking the second hit and sending it to the opponent as a hard-driven attack, a tip, or an off-speed attack. This allows the team to attack from all three positions. Furthermore, it is advantageous to have a left-handed setter because it is easier for such a setter to attack on-hand.

Why Are the 6-2 and 5-1 Offenses Important?

The 6-2 offense is important because it allows a team an additional option for its attack. This means that teams can formulate and run a system of plays that includes various combinations of players and movement of players to different parts of the net. This concept of developing a system of plays is very advanced and beyond the scope of this book. Most of these combination plays are based on the ability of the middle attacker to hit a quick set. A quick set is set immediately in front of the setter and only about 1 foot above the top of the net.

The 5-1 offense is the best offense for any team that has only one setter. Many coaches feel that this offense is the best and most efficient because every attacker hits the sets of only one setter. Attackers do not have to worry about a second setter who has different timing in the sets.

The setter can also attack when in the front row; therefore, more options are available on the second contact. The setter must also be an extremely good blocker. Teams with a short setter are at a disadvantage when the setter is in the front row. Shorter players can be very effective spikers if the ball is set off the net, but it is very difficult for them to block unless they are excellent jumpers.

When using the 5-1 offense, a team can also employ a variety of serve reception patterns that attempt to hide the front row or back row status of the setter. Some opposing teams forget to watch for this and are surprised when the setter attacks the ball on the second contact as a front row player, because they are thinking that the setter is in the back row. This option can often be extremely effective.

How to Execute the 6-2 and 5-1 Offenses

The main differences between the serve reception W-formation for the simple offenses and for the multiple offenses involve two players. In the multiple offenses, the setter is a back row player and does not receive serve—all three front row players are involved in serve reception. The center back player receives serve in the deep court rather than in frontcourt (Diagram 10.1).

Once a team has mastered the International 4-2 and 6-2 offensive systems, learning the 5-1 is fairly simple. The 5-1 combines the actions of these two other offenses, actually using each one for half of the total rotations. During three rotations, the setter is a back row player, and formations are the same as in the 6-2. During the other three rotations, the setter is a front row player, and the formations are the same as the International 4-2.

Serve Reception

The W-formation for serve reception can be used with the 6-2. The setter is a back row player and therefore must initially hide behind a front row player rather than in a position close to the net. When the setter is the right back or center back player, the movement to the net is easy because the distance is short. However, when the setter is in the left back position, the movement is difficult because the distance is rather long. The setter should initiate movement to the net the instant the ball is contacted on the serve. The remaining five players assume fairly normal positions, with the three forwards as the front line of the W and the two backs as the back line. Refer to Diagrams 10.2, 10.3, and 10.4 for the alignments used when the setter is in the three back row positions.

The setter moves to the net, taking a position to the right of center front between the right forward and center forward attackers. The setter faces the left side, the strong side, of the court. Refer to the

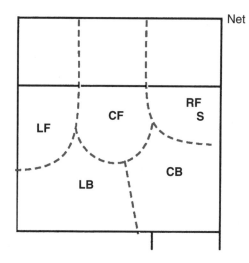

Diagram 10.1 Serve-reception responsibilities, W-formation, setter is RB, 6-2 offense.

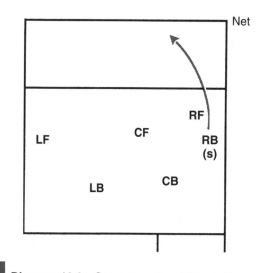

Diagram 10.2 Serve reception, W-formation, setter is RB, 6-2 offense.

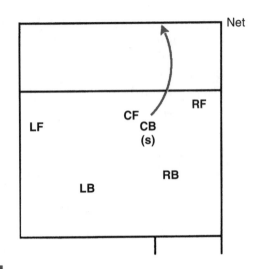

Diagram 10.3 Serve reception, W-formation, setter is CB, 6-2 offense.

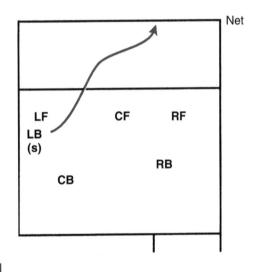

Diagram 10.4 Serve reception, W-formation, setter is LB, 6-2 offense.

diagrams to view the pattern of movement for the setter coming from each of the three back row positions. Note that when the setter is the left back, the distance to move is the greatest. When moving to the net from this position, the setter must keep his or her eyes on the receivers as the ball is passed (see Diagram 10.4).

When the setter is in the back row in the 5-1, the W-formation serve reception pattern is exactly the same as in the 6-2 offense. The setter hides behind a front row player and moves to the net as soon as the ball is contacted on the serve, remembering to keep the eyes on the receivers at all times. The setter must be in a set position when receiving the pass. The set-

ter then directs the offense and follows the set to cover the attack. After covering, the setter returns to the right back position on the court and prepares to defend against an attack by the opponent.

When the setter is a front row player, the serve reception is the same as that used in the International 4-2. The setter can take a position at the net or in such a manner that it appears as if the setter is penetrating from a back row position to the net. Diagrams 10.5, 10.6, and 10.7 show the second method of lining up when the setter is a front row player and the team attempts to disguise that fact.

When the setter attempts to disguise his or her location, the setter must make sure not to overlap

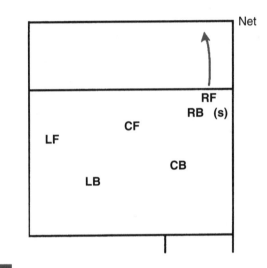

Diagram 10.5 Serve reception, setter is RF, using 5-1 offense.

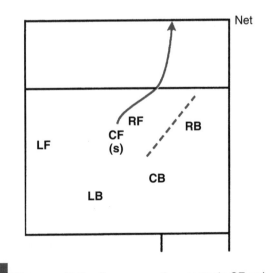

Diagram 10.6 Serve reception, setter is CF, using 5-1 offense.

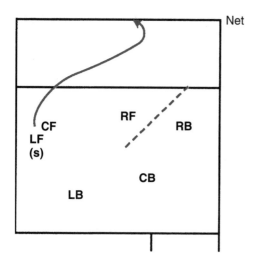

Diagram 10.7 Serve reception, setter is LF, using 5-1 offense.

the player next to that position. Once the ball is contacted on the serve, the setter assumes the right forward position and remains there until the next serve.

Covering the Attacker

In the 6-2 offense, covering the attacker can be accomplished with the same three-player semicircle and two players back, as used in the simple offenses. However, the alignment of these players is much different from the previous offenses. When covering in the 6-2, the setter is in the middle of the three-player semicircle. The center forward is the player closest to the net.

Refer to Diagrams 10.8, 10.9, and 10.10 for the

Summary of Player Responsibilities for Successful Serve Reception

All Players

- decide who will receive the ball as soon as possible after contact by the server,
- call for the ball before it crosses the plane of the net,
- open up to the player playing the ball, and
- help call the ball out-of-bounds for other players.

Front Row Players

- allow balls that are higher then chest level to be played by back row players,
- do not move back more than one step to play the ball,
- call the ball out on the sideline for the back row player on the same side of the court, and
- be ready to move forward quickly on short serves.

Back Row Players

- allow a ball that is chest height or higher to go out-of-bounds,
- call the ball out on the sideline for the front row player on the same side of the court,
- are more aggressive from the left back position in receiving when the ball is between the left and right backs,
- call the ball out over the end line for the other back, and
- always position themselves between the front row players.

Setters

- never receive the serve,
- call short serves,
- call for the pass and extend hand closer to the net high as a target for the passer, and
- face the left sideline with the right foot forward in the stride position.

Setters (Back Row)

- move to the net as soon as the ball is contacted on the serve,
- hide behind a front row player to prevent server from serving at them, and
- keep eyes on the receiver and the pass when moving from the left back position.

alignment of players covering the attacker in all three attacking positions when the setter is the right back. When the setter is in the left back and center back positions for serve reception, he or she—after penetrating to the net, setting, and moving to cover the attacker—returns to the right back position and remains there until the next serve. The setter specializes as a right back because it is easiest to move to the net from this position. It is also an area less likely to be attacked by the opponent because it is the power alley for their weak side. If the setter does not have to dig the ball defensively, the setter is available to

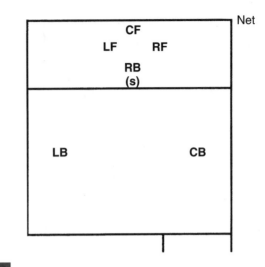

Diagram 10.10 Spike coverage, CF is spiking, multiple offense.

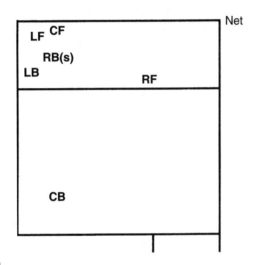

Diagram 10.8 Spike coverage, LF is spiking, multiple offense.

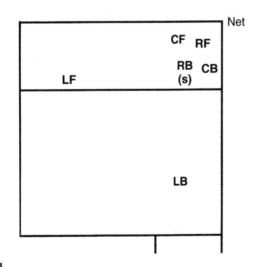

Diagram 10.9 Spike coverage, RF is spiking, multiple offense.

direct the attack.

The center forward covers in a position close to the net because it is assumed that this player is moving to the net for a quick set on every serve reception. If the center forward does not go to the net for a quick attack, the setter finds it difficult to move to a covering position without running into that player.

In the 5-1 offensive system, covering the attacker is the same as it is for the 6-2 offense when the setter is in the back row, and identical to the International 4-2 offense when the setter is in the front row (refer to the 6-2 and International 4-2). The 3-2 coverage is used, with the three-person semicircle around the attacker and two players filling the spaces in the backcourt.

Free Ball

In free ball movement in the 6-2, all three attackers move off the net to the attack line, and the setter quickly penetrates to the net from the right back position. The center back must adjust positioning to the right back point of the W. The setter must communicate the free ball call to all teammates but particularly to the center back. If the center back is unaware that a free ball has been called and does not adjust positioning, the right back area of the court is open and extremely vulnerable. When passing a free ball to the setter, the receivers should use an overhead pass, whenever possible, and turn their shoulders in the direction of the pass (see Diagram 10.11).

As for free ball and covering the attacker, the pattern continues: The free ball formation in the 5-1 offense is identical to the formation used in the 6-2 offense when the setter is in the back row, and identical to the International 4-2 when the setter is in the front row (refer to the 6-2 and the International 4-2). When the setter is a front row player, the right back player must always remember to move toward the attack line as if playing a forward position. The right back position seems to be the one that is most difficult to learn.

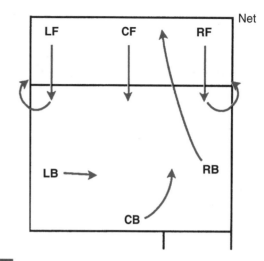

Diagram 10.11 Base defense to free ball, multiple offense, setter back row.

MULTIPLE OFFENSE SUCCESS STOPPERS

Most of the errors occurring in serve reception, coverage of the attacker, and free ball formations are due to players either leaving a position prematurely or not adjusting position soon enough. The three most common problem areas are (a) the front line players not moving off the net quickly enough on a free ball, (b) the setter penetrating to the net too soon when anticipating a free ball, and (c) the center back not adjusting to the right back area when the setter penetrates to the net.

Because the 5-1 offense is a combination of the International 4-2 and the 6-2, the errors associated with these two systems are the same as the errors for the 5-1. During the three rotations when the setter is a front row player, the errors would be the same as the errors found in the International 4-2. When the setter is penetrating from the back row for the other three rotations, the errors would be the same as found in the 6-2.

ERROR	CORRECTION
Setter in Front Row	
1. The setter receives the serve.	1. Setter should hide at the net and not receive the serve under any circumstances.
2. A free ball falls between a front row player and a back row player.	2. The two forwards must move quickly off the net to the attack line and assume a ready position before the opponent makes contact with a ball that is being sent over the net.
3. The ball rebounds off the opponent's block and falls to the floor on the attacker's side.	3. Three players must assume a coverage position around the attacker.
4. A player in the W-formation gets hit on the back by a passed ball.	4. All players must open up to the receiver by turning and facing that player.

ERROR	CORRECTION
5. The serve falls to the court between two players.	5. Receivers must call for the serve prior to the ball's crossing the net.
6. The ball rebounds off the block and falls to the court between the coverage and the sideline.	6. The player covering the line should have the outside foot on the sideline and should not play any ball that rebounds off the block beyond the sideline side of the body.
7. The attacker prevents the coverage from playing the ball.	7. The attacker should not play a ball that rebounds off the block unless it stays between the attacker and the net.
8. A free ball falls to the court in the right forward position.	8. The setter is the right forward and remains at the net; therefore, the right back must adjust and cover this area of the court.
9. The setter attempts to back set.	9. The two eligible attackers are in the center forward and left forward positions; there is no right forward attacker.

Setter in Back Row

ERROR	CORRECTION
1. A pass or dig reaches the net before the setter.	1. In receiving service, the setter must move to the net as soon as the serve is contacted; defending against an attack, the setter must move to the net from a defensive position as soon as it is evident that the attack will not be to the right back area.
2. The attack lands in the right back position with no one to receive it.	2. The setter must realize that the primary responsibility is defense and that the secondary responsibility is to direct the attack.
3. The setter and the center forward collide when trying to cover an attacker.	3. The center forward must charge to the net for a possible quick attack on each offensive series. If the center forward does not charge to the net, the setter will collide with this player as they both move to cover.
4. A free ball falls between the front row players and the back row players.	4. All three forwards must move quickly to the attack line, set themselves, and be prepared to play a free ball.
5. A third ball over the net lands in the right back position with no one to play it.	5. The setter must communicate the free ball call to all teammates. The center back must adjust when the setter penetrates to the net.
6. The serve falls to the court between the two back row players in the W.	6. The left back player should be the aggressive player on serve reception when the serve is between the two back players.

MULTIPLE OFFENSE

DRILLS

1. Serve Reception and Attack

In this drill you practice receiving serve, setting up, and covering your attacker. The setter can use any of three options.

A team of six lines up on one side of the court, with a server on the opposite side of the court (see Diagram a). The server serves underhand to the receiving team. Using a W-formation with the setter in the right back position, the team receives the serve, executes an attack with any of the three front row attackers, and covers the attacker (see Diagram b). The ball must land within the boundaries of the opposite court for the attack to be considered successful.

The team receives five good serves, then rotates one position. Drill continues until players have rotated around to their original starting positions.

Success Goal = 24 successful receptions of serve to a completed attack out of 30 serves ___

Success Check
• Call ball early ___
• Set position before playing ball ___
• Setter should indicate location to which receiver should pass ball ___

To Increase Difficulty
• Serve harder and lower.
• Vary the serves.
• Serve the seams.
• The setter is told whom to set as he or she receives the pass.

To Decrease Difficulty
• Serve directly to the receiver.
• Serve high and easy.
• Set to only one person for all five serves in rotation.

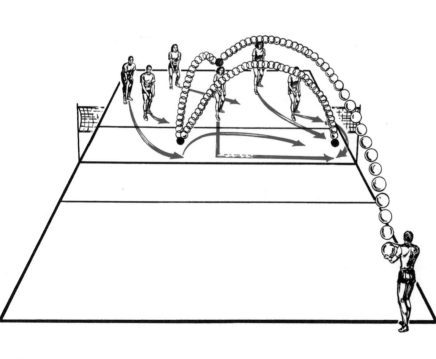

a

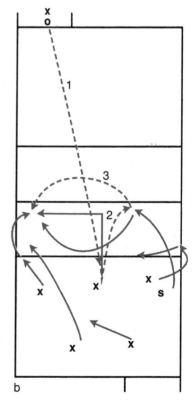

b

2. Free Ball and Attack

In this drill you are to practice your movement off the net in preparation for receiving a free ball from your opponent. The movement should first be straight back. Then, after recognizing you will not pass, you should wing out to prepare for your approach.

Three attackers, a setter, and a passer set up on one side of the net, and a tosser stands on the opposite side. The three attackers begin in the three front row positions in the base defensive formation. The setter begins in the right back of the court. The passer begins in the left back position.

The tosser yells "free" and tosses the ball to the passer. The passer passes to the setter, who has penetrated to the net. At the free ball call, the attackers drop back to the attack line and prepare to hit. The setter sets to one of the three attackers, who makes a successful attack. All players should cover as appropriate. The team receives 15 free balls.

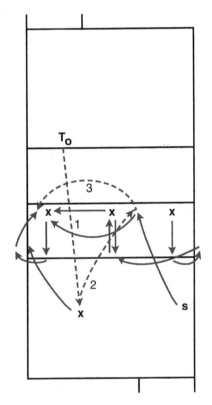

Success Goal = 12 completed attacks in 15 attempts ___

✔ Success Check

• Quick movement to attack line ___
• Angle shoulders toward direction of pass ___
• Wing out after pass is completed ___
• Setter moves to net as soon as free ball is called ___

To Increase Difficulty

• Toss low and hard.
• Shorten time between the free ball signal and the toss.
• Tosser indicates the attacker as the ball is being passed to the setter.

To Decrease Difficulty

• Increase time between the free ball signal and the toss.
• Toss high, easy balls to the receivers.
• Tosser indicates to whom the toss will be made.

3. Setter Penetration and Right Back Covering

In this drill the setter practices penetrating to the net from a back court, defensive position after calling "free ball." The center back must move from the base defensive position to cover the area vacated by the setter.

A middle and an outside attacker, a setter, and a center back player set up on one side of the net. A tosser stands on the opposite side of the net.

The tosser yells "free" and tosses the ball to the right back corner of the opposite court. At the "free" signal, the setter repeats "free," penetrates to the net, and the center back moves quickly to cover the right back area of the court. The center back passes to the setter, who sets to the middle or outside hitters to complete the successful attack. The team receives 15 free balls.

Success Goal =

the center back must pass 12 out of 15 free balls
  to the setter ___

the group must complete 10 out of 12 attacks ___

Success Check

• Setter's free ball signal is essential ___
• Center back moves quickly to position ___
• Accurate passing and setting ___

To Increase Difficulty

• Vary the direction and location of the toss within
  the right back area of the court.
• Toss the ball hard.
• Shorten time between the free ball signal and
  the toss.

To Decrease Difficulty

• Lengthen the time between free ball signal and
  the toss.
• Toss the ball higher and easier.
• Toss to the same spot every time.

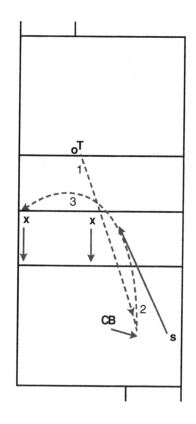

4. Set, Cover, and Recover

In this drill the setter practices penetrating to the net from a defensive position, setting the high outside set, moving to cover the attacker, and quickly returning to the defensive position. Outside hitters practice attacking.

Have three setters in the right back position, a passer in the left back position, and three hitters in the left front position on one side of the court. A tosser on the opposite side of the court yells "free" and tosses the ball over the net to the passer. The passer passes the ball to a setter who has penetrated to the setter's position at the net. The setter sets the ball high outside to the attacker. The setter must follow the set by moving to the coverage position, arriving there before the attacker contacts the ball. As always, the ball must land within the boundaries of the other side on the attack.

After the ball is attacked, the setter quickly returns to the end of the setting line in the right back position, and the attacker goes to the end of the attack line. The tosser immediately tosses the next ball to the passer, and the play is repeated with the second setter and second attacker. The team receives 15 tosses.

Success Goal =
12 good sets and coverages out of 15 ___
12 successful attacks out of 15 ___

✔ Success Check
- Indicate target ___
- Set ball and follow to coverage ___
- Touch floor with hands ___
- Backpedal to right back position ___

To Increase Difficulty
- Vary the direction and force of the toss.
- Set the ball lower to the outside hitter.

To Decrease Difficulty
- Toss directly at the passer.
- Setter starts at the net.
- Setter sends higher sets to the attacker.

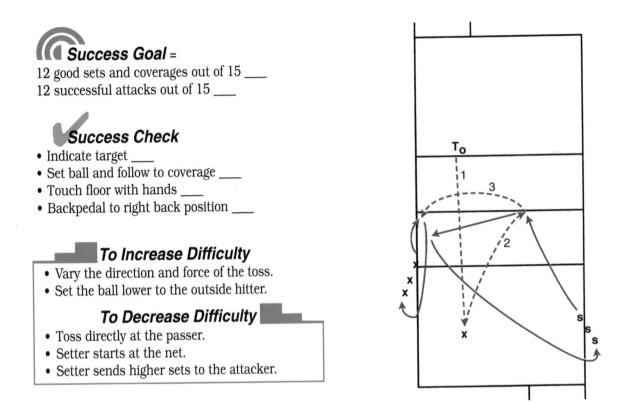

5. Free Ball

The purpose of this drill is to work as a team to develop total court movement during the reception of a free ball. All members of the team must move in unison for success.

A team of six lines up on one side of the court. The three forwards are at the net in blocking position. The center back is in the center of the court, and the left and right backs are on their respective sidelines 20 feet from the net.

A tosser on the opposite side of the net yells "free," delays for a couple of seconds, then tosses the ball over the net high and easy. The team of six quickly moves into the W-formation, receives the ball, sets an attack, and covers the attacker.

The team receives five balls, then rotates one position. Continue this drill until the players have rotated to their original starting positions.

Success Goal = 24 out of 30 successful
attacks with the proper coverage ___

✔ Success Check
- Move quickly to attack line ___
- Set position before playing ball ___
- Square shoulders to direction of pass ___
- Keep low posture on coverage ___

To Increase Difficulty
- Toss various heights and locations.
- Toss the ball quicker after yelling "free."

To Decrease Difficulty
- Start in the free ball position.
- Toss to a designated receiver.
- Toss at a consistent height.

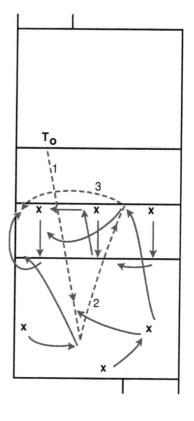

6. Cover and Dig

In this drill the team moves to cover the attacker and practices playing a ball after the block. This drill can be continuous as long as you have successful attacks, blocks, and digs. See how long you can keep it going for each attack.

A team of six sets up on one side of the court in the W-formation, with the setter in the center forward position. On the opposite side of the net, two blockers stand on a box on the right side of the court.

A tosser on the same court as the blockers yells "free" and throws a high ball over the net. The team receives the free ball, sets an attack to their left forward, and covers. The blockers block the ball, and the coverage attempts to dig successfully, which means being able to set up for a second attack.

The team receives five tosses, then rotates one position. This drill continues until the players have returned to their original positions.

Success Goal = 18 out of 30 successful digs off the opposing blocks ___

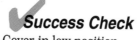

Success Check
- Cover in low position ___
- Dig ball high ___
- Cover second attack ___
- Blockers must keep ball in play ___

To Increase Difficulty

- Toss with various heights and directions.
- Shorten the time between the free ball call and the toss.

To Decrease Difficulty

- Toss high, easy, and directly at the player.
- Lengthen the time between calling "free" and tossing.
- The setter sets higher.

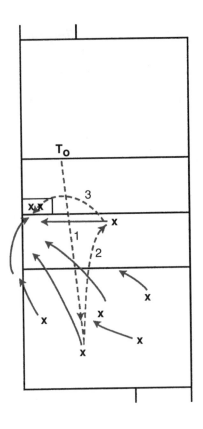

7. Serve and Free Ball

This drill simulates a game situation of receiving serve, making a successful attack, covering the attacker, moving quickly to base defense, receiving a free ball from the opponent, and attacking again. This movement happens continuously in a game setting.

A team of six starts in a W-formation. A tosser and a server are on the opposite side of the net, each with a ball.

The server serves. The receiving team passes the serve, sets an attack, and covers (see Diagram a, next page).

The team immediately assumes starting positions, as shown in Diagram b, next page. The tosser calls "free" and tosses the ball high over the net. The receiving team passes the free ball, sets an attack, and covers.

Play continues with another serve, followed by another free ball. The team receives five good serves alternating with five free balls, then rotates one position. The drill continues until all players rotate around to their starting positions.

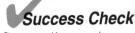

Success Goal =

24 out of 30 successful attacks off serves with the correct coverage ___

24 out of 30 successful attacks off free balls with the correct coverage ___

Success Check

- Cover entire court ___
- Call ball as soon as possible ___
- Set coverage before attacker contacts ball ___
- Move to base defense ___

To Increase Difficulty

- Use any method of serving.
- Serve the seams.
- Vary the height and force of toss.
- Shorten the time between yelling "free" and tossing the ball.

To Decrease Difficulty

- Serve underhand.
- Serve directly to the receiver.
- Wait longer between yelling "free" and tossing the ball.

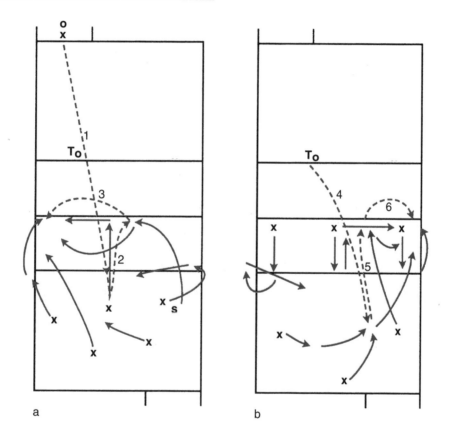

a   b

8. Setter Attacks Second Ball

When using the 5-1, the setter is a front row player for three rotations and is an eligible attacker. An attack by the setter is very effective in catching the opponents off guard. In this drill the setter practices attacking the pass.

On one side of the court place a passer in the left back position and a setter in the right front position. A tosser and a blocker (left front) are on the opposite court.

The tosser tosses the ball over the net to the passer. The passer passes the ball to the setter, who attacks the ball using an off-speed spike, a hard-driven spike, or a tip. Off-speed hits should be directed past the blocker toward the center of the opponent's court; tips should go toward the center of the court close to the net or to the sideline behind the left front blocker. Setter attacks 15 passes.

Success Goal = 10 out of 15 successful attacks ___

✔ **Success Check**

- Disguise setter intent ___
- Vary attack ___
- Go over or past block ___
- Make off-speed attack drop quickly ___
- Be prepared for opponent's blocking ___

To Increase Difficulty

- Vary the throw's force and height.
- Pass with varying heights to the setter.

To Decrease Difficulty

- Toss the ball high and easy to the passer.
- Allow sufficient time between tosses.
- Pass the ball high to the setter.

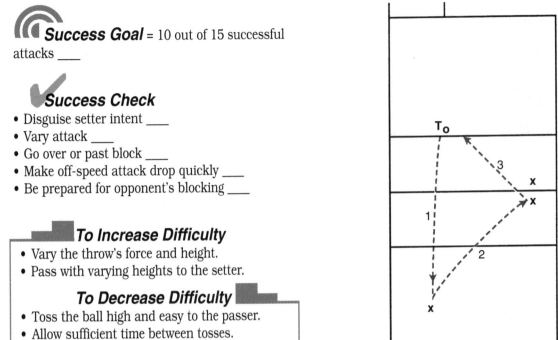

MULTIPLE OFFENSE SUCCESS SUMMARY

If your team has at least six players who can attack effectively, you can use either a 6-2 or a 5-1 multiple offense. Using a back row player as setter allows you to have more options with three front row players eligible to attack.

Have a skilled observer analyze your team's movement on free ball, serve reception, and attacker coverage to determine if all players are moving into the correct formations based on Diagrams 10.1 through 10.11.

STEP 11

2-4 DEFENSE: OPTION ATTACK

STOPPING THE MULTIPLE

You are playing your arch rival, a powerful spiking team that loves to attack the ball with great force and seldom uses off-speed spikes or tips. The setter is good and uses all the attack options available to her. Your block is not closing well and the middle back portion of the court is vulnerable. You decide to change to a 2-4 defense to better cover the court.

The 2-4 defense is one of the two most frequently used defenses in volleyball, along with the 2-1-3 defense. The 2-4 defense is more difficult to execute because each player is required to receive two different types of attacks, both the tip and the hard-driven spike. The success of this defense thus relies heavily on the ability of the players to read the play of the opponent. The 2-1-3 defense is often the first one used by a team. Many teams are capable of executing both of these defensive systems and employ the one that proves more successful against a given opponent. However, it is better to be able to execute one defensive system effectively than to try to use both before either is mastered.

Why Is the 2-4 Defense Important?

Generally, as the level of play in volleyball improves, teams are capable of executing more powerful attacks. The 2-1-3 defense becomes less efficient as the attack becomes more powerful. The 2-4 defense allows a team to cover the deep court more completely and thus is usually employed against a team with a more powerful attack.

In the 2-4 defense, a player is positioned in the backcourt behind the block. Protecting this area allows a team to dig balls that are deflected by the block high to the backcourt as well as balls that go through the block. This added protection is especially needed against opponents who utilize a quick middle attack. Often a middle blocker, due to the threat of a middle attack, does not have time to close the block, thus leaving the middle backcourt vulnerable. The extra backcourt player covers this area.

How to Execute the 2-4 Defense

As in the 2-1-3 defense, there are two basic positions to take when executing the 2-4 defense. The base defensive formation is used when your team is waiting to see what play the opponent will execute. If the opponent is able to execute a spike, your team can counter with a block. If the opponent is unable to attack, your team should drop back into the free ball formation (discussed in Steps 8 and 10 on offense). All players on your team must move into the same formation. Usually the setter indicates whether your team should block or move to receive a free ball. Sometimes the setter calls a free ball and the opponent, in fact, completes a hard-driven spike. If this happens and all members of your team have assumed the same formation, the court is still sufficiently covered.

Base

The base defensive formation with the 2-4 is slightly different from that with the 2-1-3. The center back player remains deep in the court and the left back and the right back players remain 5 feet from the sidelines. In the 2-4 alignment, the center back player is positioned on the end line. The starting position for the center back must be deeper than in the 2-1-3 to enhance the ability of this player to attain that deep position. The left and right backs adjust their positions about 3 to 5 feet in from the sideline to cover the center of the court. If this adjustment isn't made, the center of the court is vulnerable to a *setter dump*—a ball placed over the net by the setter on second contact. Refer to Diagram 11.1 for the correct base defensive position for using the 2-4 defense.

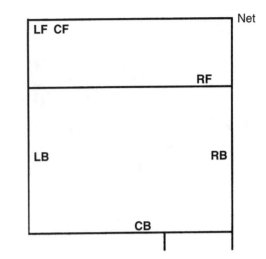

Diagram 11.2 The 2-4 defense against the spike by the opposing RF.

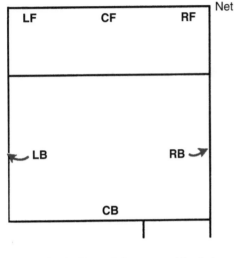

Diagram 11.1 Base defense used for 2-4 defense.

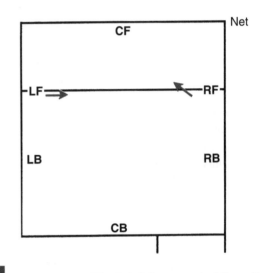

Diagram 11.3 The 2-4 defense against the spike by the opposing CF.

Block

As soon as the location of the opponent's attack is determined, the defending team sets the block and defensive coverage. In the 2-4 defensive system, location of the four backcourt players and their responsibilities are different than in the 2-1-3. Refer to Diagrams 11.2, 11.3, and 11.4 for correct defensive positioning for attacks from all three opposing forwards.

In the 2-4 defensive alignment, each player has to be prepared to receive any kind of attack. This makes reading the opponent's play extremely important. *Reading* is the ability to intelligently anticipate what the opponent is going to do. The responsibilities of all players are now described for the defense against a right forward attack from the opponent (see Dia-

gram 11.2 and 11.5). The left back takes a position on the line and is responsible for tips over the block, spikes down-the-line, and off-speed attacks toward the center of the court. The left back should be more aggressive than the right back in defending this center court area. The left back can cover two thirds of the court width, leaving the remaining third to the right back.

The center back remains deep on the end line and is responsible for spikes over the top of the block, spikes deflected by the block, and high, easy balls to either deep corner of the court.

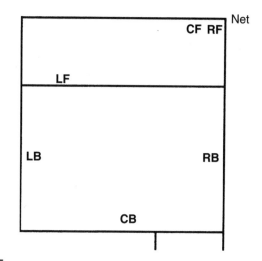

Diagram 11.4 The 2-4 defense against the spike by the opposing LF.

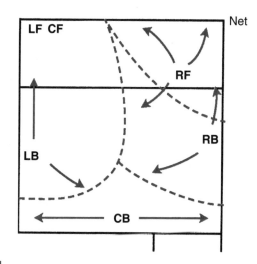

Diagram 11.5 The 2-4 defense against the spike by the opposing RF, showing player responsibilities for each position.

The right back is in the power alley and is responsible for hard-driven spikes that go by the block. The right back lines up with the inside shoulder of the center blocker, with the attacker's hand and ball in view. The right back is also responsible for off-speed attacks to the center of the court and toward the right third of the court.

The right forward moves off the net to the attack line and 10 feet in from the sideline. This player is responsible for tips to the center of the court close to the net, sharp-angled spikes, and junk off the net.

The responsibilities of all players in aligning to defend against the left forward attacker are basically the same. The players' roles are determined by their positions on the court. The right back takes a position on the line and is responsible for tips over the block, spikes down-the-line, and off-speed attacks toward the center of the court. The left back is in the power alley and is responsible for hard-driven spikes that go by the block and off-speed attacks to the center of the court. The center back remains deep on the end line and is responsible for spikes over the top of the block, spikes deflected by the block, and high, easy balls to either deep corner of the court. The left forward moves off the net to the attack line and 10 feet in from the sideline. This player is responsible for tips to the center of the court close to the net, sharp-angled spikes, and junk off the net.

In the defense against the center attack, because only one blocker is used, five players cover the backcourt. Both off-blockers move to the attack line and have the responsibilities just described.

Player Responsibilities Summary for Successful Block Defense

All Players

- should anticipate play of opponent by attempting to read what the opponent will do and
- move to the defensive position, set, and be ready to react before the ball is contacted by the attacker.

Front Row Players

- should have hands at shoulder level or higher in starting position,
- should move along the net left and right but never away from the net and back to the net,
- have no arm swing,
- put hands across net on the block, and
- when playing the off-blocker, move to the attack line ready to play defense.

Backcourt Players

- keep low body posture with weight forward on the toes and
- move through the ball toward the target.

Off-Blocker

- plays tips to the center of the court,
- plays junk off the net, and
- plays hard-driven spikes at the sharp angle to the sideline.

Center Back

- must stay deep in the court on or behind the end line,
- is responsible for any ball that hits the block and rebounds deep into the court,
- plays any high balls to the corners of the court behind the two line players, and
- must react by moving forward to cover the middle of the court if the blocker does not close the block.

Defensive Players on Line

- must play any spike down-the-line and
- must be ready to move forward and dig any tip over the block directed down-the-line.

Power Alley Player

- aligns so that the inside shoulder of the middle blocker, the ball, and the attacker's hand are all in view and
- receives spikes or off-speeds into the power alley.

2-4 DEFENSE SUCCESS STOPPERS

The most common errors a team makes when executing the 2-4 defense are associated with the players' inability to determine who should play the ball. You should not decide in advance who should play the ball; you should simply react to the play as it develops. Players are positioned on the court in such a way that when two of you move to the ball at the same time, one should always be in front of the other, and you should cross rather than collide. Concern about colliding with a teammate may cause you to stop rather than play through the ball.

ERROR	CORRECTION
1. The center back player attempts to dig an off-speed attack to the middle of the court.	1. The center back player must remain deep on the end line; the left back or right back is responsible for off-speed attacks to this area.
2. A ball dug by the setter does not get set.	2. The setter, after digging the attack, is not eligible to make the second contact or set; in this situation the player in the right forward position assumes the setting role.
3. The tip over the block falls to the court without being dug.	3. The player on the sideline on the same side of the block is responsible for spikes down-the-line and tips over the block.
4. The line player behind the block ducks when a spike down-the-line is chest high or higher.	4. The line player must play this spike, even if just by raising the arms and blocking it.
5. A deep tip falls to either back corner of the court.	5. The center back is responsible for covering deep, easy balls to both corners of the court.
6. A spiked ball goes through the block and hits the floor.	6. If the middle blocker doesn't close the block, the center back must move forward in anticipation of a spike to the center of the court.

2-4 DEFENSE

DRILLS

1. Six-Player Defense

In this drill a team defends using a 2-4 defense against an attack from any of the three attacking positions—left, center, or right. The defending team reacts according to the position of the attack and also according to the type of attack—spike or free ball. The defense tries to complete an attack in transition.

A team of six sets up on one side of the court in base defensive position. A tosser, setter, and three attackers set up on the opposite side.

The tosser overhand tosses the ball to the setter, who sets any of the attackers. The setter should disguise which attacker will be set, so that the defense must react to the attack as though in a game. The attacker spikes, tips, or off-speed spikes over the net.

The defending team must either block the spike, or receive it and attempt to execute a counterattack. If the attacking players are unable to spike, the defending team should move to a free ball position to receive the third hit over. When the defending team successfully makes the transition and executes the attack, they must cover the attacker.

The defending team should receive five attacks, then rotate one position. Continue until all players are back in their original positions.

 **Success Goal** = 20 successful blocks or digs and counterattacks out of 30 spikes ___

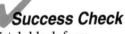 **Success Check**
- Watch for direction of set ___
- Move to appropriate beginning defensive positions ___
- Read attack and react to ball ___
- Prepare for attack on transition ___

To Increase Difficulty
- Vary height and location of the toss.
- Set the ball lower to the attacker.

To Decrease Difficulty
- Toss high, easy, and directly at the setter.
- Attackers tell the defense who will spike.
- Defenders tell attackers where to spike.

2. Digging the Power Attack

In this drill the spiker attempts to simulate a game situation by using a variety of directions and speeds of attack. The defensive team practices successfully receiving these attacks.

A team of six sets up on one side of the court. On the other side, a spiker in the left front position stands on a box with a feeder alongside.

The spiker self-tosses the ball high enough to allow the middle blocker to join the outside blocker, then attacks cross-court. The team attempts to dig the spike and complete an attack transition. The ball must land inbounds on the attack.

As usual, the drill is run with five spikes, followed by the team rotating one position.

Success Goal =
20 good digs out of 30 spikes ___
15 completed attacks out of 30 spikes ___

Success Check
- Watch block form ___
- Position outside block ___
- Keep ball and opposing attacker's arm in view ___
- Back to sideline ___
- Read attack and react ___

To Increase Difficulty
- Spiker self-tosses the ball lower.
- Vary direction and speed of the spike.

To Decrease Difficulty
- Spiker indicates direction of attack.
- Spiker self-tosses the ball higher.
- The middle blocker begins in a joined position.

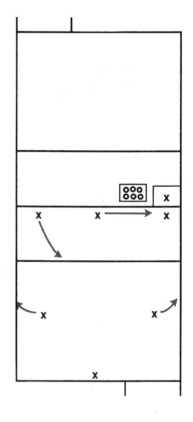

3. Setter Digs and Right Forward Sets

The back row setter on defense is often required to play the first ball over the net. In this case, the right forward should assume the setting role. This drill allows players to practice this situation.

Use the same formation as the previous drill. Here, though, the left forward on the box spikes down-the-line. This forces the right back (setter) to dig the ball, which means that another player must set. It is preferable that the right forward sets in this situation.

This drill is run with five spikes before the team rotates one position.

 **Success Goal** =
20 out of 30 successful digs ___
15 out of 30 completed attacks ___

Success Check
- Setter digs ball high ___
- Setter signals he or she has played first ball ___
- Right forward or closest player calls for ball ___
- High, easy sets used in transition ___
- Complete transition attack by covering ___

To Increase Difficulty

- The spiker uses a lower self-toss to force receivers to react more quickly.
- The spiker varies the direction and force of the attack.

To Decrease Difficulty

- The spiker tells the setter what type of attack will be executed.
- The spiker indicates the direction in which the attack will be executed.
- The spiker uses a higher self-toss.

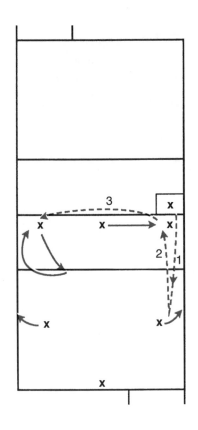

4. Covering Cross-Court Tips

In this drill the team practices receiving tips to the center of the court by the opponent and setting up an attack in transition. The left forward needs to practice moving in to receive the tip and then quickly winging out to prepare for an attack.

This drill uses the same formation as the previous two drills. Now, though, the left forward on the box tips the ball toward the center of the court close to the net. The left forward of the opposing team should dig this tip.

This drill runs with five tips followed by the team rotating.

Success Goal =
20 out of 30 successful digs ___
15 out of 30 completed attacks ___

Success Check
- Quickly move to ball ___
- Get into low position ___
- Dig ball high and to center of court ___
- Cover every time ___

To Increase Difficulty
- Shorten the time between tips.
- Tip the ball with less height and distance.

To Decrease Difficulty
- Tip the ball higher and farther.
- Attacker self-tosses the ball higher.
- Lengthen the time between tips.

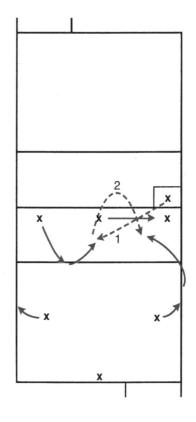

5. Digging Deep Tips to the Right Back Corner

In this drill the team practices digging deep tips by the opponent to the right back corner. The deep defensive player is responsible for moving to the corner to receive this ball behind the right back. In a multiple offense, the right back is the setter and should quickly move to the net to set the ball in transition.

This drill uses the same formation as the three previous drills. However, the left forward tips or passes the ball high to the right back corner of the opposing court. The center back defensive player should dig this ball as the setter penetrates to the net.

This drill is run with five tips or passes; then the team rotates.

 **Success Goal** =
20 out of 30 successful digs ___
15 out of 30 completed attacks ___

Success Check
- Move to ball ___
- Set position ___
- Dig ball high toward center of court ___
- Follow set to cover ___

To Increase Difficulty
- Tip the ball lower.
- Shorten the time between tips.
- Mix in more hard-driven spikes.

To Decrease Difficulty
- Attacker tips the ball higher.
- The attacker lengthens the time between tips.

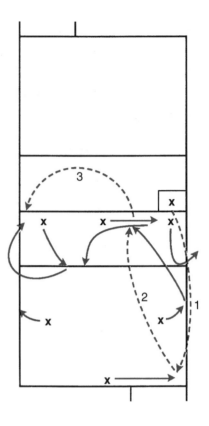

2-4 DEFENSE SUCCESS SUMMARY

During a scrimmage, have a skilled observer watch your team practicing the 2-4 defense. The observer should check to see if your team assumes the base defensive formation as soon as you send the ball over the net to the opponent. It is helpful if a team leader is selected to call the formation. "Base" is called as soon as the ball is returned to the opponent, "free ball" is called if the opponent does set up for a spike, and "block" will be called if the opponent spikes. The observer should check first for the selection of the correct formation and then to be sure every player assumes the correct position (see Diagrams 11.1 through 11.5).

STEP 12

GAME SITUATIONS: FOCUSING YOUR EFFORTS

Now that you have mastered all the basic skills and several options for offensive and defensive strategies, you are ready to play a legal game against an opponent. Of course, your team needs to make several decisions before the competition begins.

1. What offensive system are you going to use?
2. What defensive system will you try?
3. Who will be your setters?
4. Who are your strongest attackers, servers, and defensive players?
5. What are the strengths of your opponent?
6. Who will be your court leader to call and direct play?

Your choice of offense depends on the equality and type of players that make up your team. If you have only four strong spikers, then a 4-2 offense is the best choice. If you have six, then a 6-2 offense would offer more options. If you wish to use a 6-2, your setters must be quick and mobile.

Defensively, you need tall, good blockers to use a 2-1-3. If you have a weak defensive player or a slow setter, the 2-1-3 is an excellent choice because the weak player or setter can be placed behind the block and will not have to receive a spiked ball.

The setters must have exceptional setting ability and must be able to assume leadership roles. A setter is often selected as the player who will call the court movements for the team.

The coach should submit a lineup with all the players in strategic starting positions. You would like to have your best server serving first. You also want your best attacker in the left forward or left back position because someone starting there would be a forward for the longest time. The best defensive player

should begin in either the right forward or right back position, and your best passers should always be in the back row. The strongest setter should be the first one to assume the setting role.

You must select a court leader to direct the play on the court (refer to "Signaling for Success" later in this step). The person should be a natural leader and ready to direct the attack and defense in an aggressive manner.

Once decisions have been made on these organizational aspects of play, you are ready to begin the game. The choice of taking first serve, receiving first, or picking the starting playing area goes to the team that wins the toss; the other team chooses from the remaining selections.

Once the game is under way, all players have to make decisions constantly about where they are supposed to be and the nature of their responsibilities. Volleyball is a game of constant movement and decision making. With each contact of the ball by your own team or by your opponent, you must anticipate the upcoming result and position yourself strategically.

If you do not do this, weak or open areas will exist on your court, and you will be vulnerable to the opponent's attack. Your team is only as strong as its weakest player; as soon as an opponent discovers who that player is, they will play the ball to that player's court area. Your team must try to play all of its players in positions that enhance the strength of the entire team.

Specialization

Rotation differentiates volleyball from other sports. All players rotate to a new position on the court each time their team earns a side out. This means that each player must learn the characteristics of six different positions. This is difficult and uses much practice time because new formations must be practiced in all six rotations.

Specialization of players is a method that alleviates this problem. Players are required to remain in their correct rotational positions only until the ball is served. Then they are allowed to move to any position either on or off the court, with the exception that back row players cannot spike or block from in front of the attack line. As soon as the ball is contacted on the serve, all players may switch to their playing positions. This is usually done by the defensive team as soon as the ball is contacted on the serve and by the offensive team either after the pass or after the ball is returned over the net.

When players specialize, they each play only one position while they are in the front row and only one position while they are in the back row. Some teams like to keep the players on the same side of the court in both the front and back rows; players might play only on the left side, only in the middle, or only on the right side. Each one of these positions has certain important characteristics. The setter usually plays on the right side and must be a leader, an excellent blocker, quick, and perceptive. The left side player must be a strong, dependable hitter and a strong digger. The middle player must be a strong blocker, capable of excellent lateral movement, and able to hit a quick, low set.

Specialization allows a coach to place players where their strengths best help the team. Specialization makes it easier for players to learn court positioning because they have to learn only two positions instead of six. It also enhances efficient use of practice time because each new formation has to be practiced in only two rotations. Most highly skilled teams use specialization.

Signaling for Success

Communication among players is essential to success. Realize that actions speak louder than words; an action by a player signals an intent to a teammate. If a player does not complete an action, then a teammate cannot be expected to either. A good example of this is during serve reception. If a front line player moves as if to receive a ball, the back line player behind who observes this will assume that the forward will receive the ball even if the front line player does not call "mine"; the back player will stop moving toward the ball. This usually results in no reception, which immediately gives a point or a side out to the opponent. A player who moves to play a ball should complete the action.

On the other hand, nonverbal signals can often be used to your team's advantage. For example, a front row player who opens up to the backcourt indicates a plan not to receive the ball.

Every team must have a series of verbal signals to communicate their intentions. The following verbal signals will help your team to play as a unit. All players must know the signals and follow them:

1. Call "mine," "ball," or "I have it" when you are going to play a ball. Team members should call for every ball, but it is especially important to call for the reception of the first ball over the net.

2. Call "out" to indicate that the ball is outside the court boundaries. It is difficult for the player who has called for the ball to judge whether the ball is in or out; a nearby teammate should make the call. Players should move toward the line before calling a ball out.

3. Call "deep" or "short" to indicate whether the ball should be received by a front line player or a back line player.

4. Call "tip" when the opponent indicates it will use that type of attack.

5. Call "over" when the next hit must go over the net to the opponent.

6. Call "touch" when, as a blocker, you contact the opponent's spike, but it remains on your side to be played by your backcourt defense. Backcourt players then realize they must play a ball which is going out.

In addition to the above signals that are used by all team members, the setter will use the following specific signals. These signals are essential in helping all team members execute the same formation at the appropriate time. If the setter does not signal the play, teammates may choose to move into different positions causing areas of the court to be insufficiently covered.

1. Call "setter" when you receive the first ball over the net and, thus, cannot make the second contact or set. This tells your teammates someone else must set. This should be the right forward if possible.

2. Call "help" when you cannot make the second contact or set. The closest teammate should make the second contact.

3. Call "free" when it becomes evident that the opponent will not complete its attack.

4. Call "block" when you need to defend against the opponent's attack.

5. Call "cover" after each set to remind your teammates to cover the upcoming attack.

The setter should also signal either verbally or with a hand signal what attack will be used. There are many systems of attack and no standard numbering system in the United States. The net can be divided into seven, eight, or nine areas. The type of set is often described with two numbers. The first number refers to the area or zone of the net where the set will be placed, the second number to the height of the set. A team can establish its own play-calling system. In this book, we have concentrated on high sets so the setter would need to communicate only which attacker is about to be set.

The attacker(s) who will not be attacking must not move to coverage before the set is actually made because sometimes the setter needs to change the direction of the set due to a poor pass. Every attacker must be ready to receive a set until the ball is actually set; then they can move to the appropriate coverage.

Game Play Choices

Each time the ball comes to your team from the opponent, you have to make a decision about the best method of playing the ball to complete the transition efficiently from defense to offense. The decision on how to receive the ball depends on the type of ball that is returned to your team by the opponent. You want to be able to execute the three-hit combination—pass, set, and attack—each time you receive the ball. The first contact is important because if you control the ball on the pass, you can easily achieve a good attack.

Usually it is a disadvantage to return the ball to the opponent on the first contact. However, if the opponent returns the ball to you high, easy, and close to the net (a free ball), your team should immediately spike it back. This is a high-percentage play and usually results in a point or a side out for your team. If your team returns that type of ball to the opponent, you can expect the same response. Returning the first contact to the opponent in an easy manner is ill-advised unless you place the ball deep to either back corner of the court.

The second contact can be effectively returned to the opponent as a spike if the setter is a front row player or if an attacker has good position on the ball and can spike the pass. The attacker should communicate this intent to the setter so that a collision between the two does not occur. The setter can also effectively send the second contact over the net by tipping it. This can be done whether the setter is a front row or a back row player. The back row setter must not cross the plane of the top of the net in playing the ball over because this is an illegal play.

Completing the three-hit combination is the most effective offense and is used the majority of the time. A smart setter can constantly keep the opponent guessing by varying the attack and occasionally sending the second contact over the net. If this play is used too often, however, it becomes ineffective.

On the next page is a list of options available for each of the three contacts, with the choices listed in order of preference.

Your team can enhance its ability to make the correct game choices by anticipating the action of your opponent. If you read the opponent well, you will seldom be caught off guard. You and your teammates need to communicate constantly about any clues that you read from your opponent's play. Your team must be in position by the time the ball is contacted on the third hit by the opponent. If not in a set position at that time, you may be too late.

Offensive Skill Options

First Contact—Receiving

Serve	*Free Ball*	*Spike*	*Tip*
1. Forearm pass	1. Spike	1. Dig with two arms	1. Forearm pass
2. Dig with one arm	2. Overhead pass	2. Dig with one arm	2. Dig with two arms
3. Overhead pass (often illegal)	3. Forearm pass	3. Dig and roll, or dig and sprawl	3. Dig with one arm
			4. Dig and roll, or dig and sprawl

Second Contact—Setting the Attack or Attack Options

1. Set to a spiker
2. Spike over the net
3. Tip over the net
4. Forearm pass to a spiker

Third Contact—Attack Options

1. Spike over the net
2. Tip over the net
3. Off-speed spike over the net
4. Spike hit with no jump and good placement
5. Overhead pass to deep corners
6. Forearm pass over the net (not recommended)

Defensive Skill Responses

Receiving a Spike

Front Row Options	*Back Row Options*
1. Three- or two-person block	1. Dig the ball and keep it on your own side
2. One-person block	2. Dig the ball and send it over the net and inbounds
3. No block	
4. Free ball position	

GAME SITUATIONS

1. Converting Free Balls to Points

Often it is to a team's advantage to modify the game situation to emphasize practice and improvement in specific aspects of strategy. Several examples of this are used in the drills presented in the offensive and defensive steps. For instance, Drill 3—setter penetration and right back covering in Step 10—is set up to practice the idea of player movement and court coverage during a free ball situation. In this drill only the key players in the movement are used. This same game aspect can be practiced by modifying a typical game situation utilizing two teams of six players. This can be accomplished as follows:

Two teams line up on either side of the net. A tosser will be positioned outside the boundaries of the court on one side of the net with a generous supply of volleyballs. Both teams will begin in base defensive formation with the setter in the right back position. The tosser will yell "free," tossing the ball over the net to the right back corner of the opposite side. The team receiving the toss quickly moves into the free ball formation with the setter moving to the net and the center back moving to cover the right back area of the court. Game play will continue until the ball becomes dead. Another toss is initiated to the same team. The tosser makes a given number of tosses to one team, changes sides, and repeats the same number to the opposite team. Score can be kept by awarding 1 point to the team winning the rally.

By keeping players in the same rotational positions for an extended time, they have the opportunity to perfect their responsibilities of the rotation. This enhances learning more than a regulation game in which one team rotates with every side out.

2. Free Ball—Efficient Movement

The same procedure as in the previous game can be followed to emphasize two other aspects of the team reception of a free ball: (a) slow movement of the attackers off the net and subsequent failure to get into position soon enough to receive the free ball and (b) movement of the forwards directly into the wing out position rather than movement straight back and then winging out. To correct situation (a), the tosser would direct the ball to the attackers at the attack line; to correct situation (b), the tosser would direct the ball to either the right or left forward but more toward the center of the court than the sideline.

3. Consecutive Serve Reception

Serve five consecutive serves from one side of the net regardless of the result of the rally; then five serves by the opposite team. This process can continue for each of the six rotations. Score can be kept by awarding 1 point to the team winning the rally.

4. Defending All Attacks

To practice defense, a teacher, a coach, or a player who has excellent control of the spike hit can stand on a box in one of the two outside attack positions spiking the ball at one of the teams. The person on the box can either spike the ball to a designated position for a given number of trials or can vary the attack, direction, and type with each trial. After every five attacks, the team rotates one position. Score can be kept by awarding 1 point to the team winning the rally. The setter should avoid setting the position where the box is located.

Beach Volleyball

In recent years the game of beach volleyball has risen tremendously in popularity. Volleyball has always been a beach activity, but now sand courts are being set up all over the world. The best opportunity for United States volleyball players to compete professionally is in the beach game. Professional leagues for the six-player game have not been successful, but the formation of new leagues continues to be a possibility. Two-person beach volleyball will be added to the Olympic program in Atlanta in 1996.

The skills involved in beach volleyball are the same as the skills used in the six-player game. One major difference in the beach game is that players need to be able to perform at a high level in every individual skill, so specialization is eliminated. Teams are comprised of either two or four players, and there are no substitutions. Whether playing two-person or four-person games, players play both at the net and in the back court.

The strategies involved in two-person beach volleyball are different than the six-player game. The two-person game demands close communication between players so that each knows what to expect of the other. Opponents will know the strengths of each player and try to use this knowledge to their advantage. For example, the player who is forced to receive serve will also be the attacker. If one partner is weaker at attacking, the opponent should focus on this weakness by serving to that player. Partners should also communicate what part of the court will be protected by the blocker so that the back court player knows how to cover. Another way beach volleyball differs from the indoor game is that players must contend with the elements, including the sun, wind, and general court conditions. The rules take these factors into consideration by having players change sides after every five points.

The size of the court in beach volleyball is the same as it is in the six-player game. A key attribute of successful beach volleyball teams is the ability of both players to read the actions of their opponents. Reading their opponents' play allows a team success in covering the entire court area.

The nature of the two-person game requires strong communication between players at all times. The best way to enhance communication is to practice two on two. Two-on-two practice improves overall skill ability because each player contacts the ball frequently. Many coaches of the six-player game use the two-player game to strengthen the reading ability of their players.

GAME SITUATIONS SUCCESS SUMMARY

These modified game situations allow teams to work at a more concentrated level than possible in a regular game situation. The action is quicker and more intense. Other possibilities are limited only by creativity. When practicing offense, concentrate on serve reception, free ball reception, and spike coverage. On defense work on base defensive formation and blocking.

At this stage, you have mastered the skills and strategies of volleyball at a level that permits you to successfully participate in a competitive situation. We hope that this knowledge will help you to enjoy playing the game and stimulate your desire to continue to improve through additional practice and playing experience.

RATING YOUR GAME SUCCESS

The best place to test your new skills is within a game. Rating can be done either by yourself or by a teacher, coach, or trained partner. Included below are two recommended means of evaluation.

Self-Evaluation

Reflect back on three game performances to rate yourself. Using the checklist below, choose the response for each question that best describes your performance.

1. I typically serve
   a. to the most strategic place on the opponent's court.
   b. to the seam between two players.
   c. to the opponent's weakest player.
   d. into the opponent's court.
2. I score ___ percent on a written test covering the basic rules.
   a. 90
   b. 80
   c. 70
   d. 60
3. I score ___ percent on a written test covering concepts, techniques, and strategies.
   a. 90
   b. 80
   c. 70
   d. 60
4. When receiving serve, I typically pass the ball
   a. to the target area.
   b. to the center of the court, not perfectly, but to a location where it can be set.
   c. so that it cannot be set, causing my team to send the opponent a free ball.
   d. so poorly that the opponent is awarded an ace.

5. I compliment other players' good hits and efforts
   a. at all times.
   b. most of the time.
   c. seldom.
   d. not at all.
6. I spike
   a. to open areas of the opponent's court.
   b. between two opponents.
   c. right at the opponent's block or right at the opponent's back row defensive players.
   d. out-of-bounds or into the net.
7. When I am going to play the ball, I call for it
   a. always.
   b. most of the time.
   c. seldom.
   d. never.
8. If a teammate calls for the ball, I let that person play it
   a. always.
   b. most of the time.
   c. seldom.
   d. never.
9. When playing the second contact, I
   a. set the spiker.
   b. forearm pass to the spiker.
   c. send the ball over the net.
   d. make an error.

10. When receiving a free ball, I
    a. spike it if possible.
    b. pass it with an overhead pass to the setter.
    c. pass it with a forearm pass to the setter.
    d. send it back over the net.
11. Any time I dig a spike, I
    a. stay on my feet and use two hands.
    b. stay on my feet and use one hand.
    c. dive or roll only when it is needed.
    d. roll or dive whether I need to or not.
12. When my team is on defense, I
    a. read the opponent's play and set myself in the best defensive position.
    b. set my position at the same spot every time.
    c. get into my position late and have difficulty making the play.
    d. watch the opponent's play and never get into position.
13. When a teammate is receiving serve, I
    a. open up to the ball and then get ready for the next play.
    b. watch the ball over my shoulder and then get ready for the next play.
    c. don't watch the ball, but immediately get ready for the next play.
    d. don't watch the ball and never get ready for the next play.
14. When I am a forward and my team is receiving a free ball, I
    a. move straight back to the attack line, play the ball, or wing out to the side to get ready to hit.
    b. move straight back to the sideline, play the ball, or remain in that position.
    c. move off the court to be ready for the attack, not being concerned about playing the ball.
    d. remain at the net, turn, and watch my teammates play the ball.
15. When a teammate is spiking, I
    a. quickly move to cover the spike and set myself in a low position before the ball is spiked, ready to play the ball off the block.
    b. quickly move to cover the spike and set myself in a medium or high position before the ball is spiked, ready to play the ball off the block.
    c. move to cover the spike, but I am not set before the ball is spiked.
    d. stand in my initial position and applaud when my teammate makes a good spike.
16. When serving, I make
    a. 9 successful serves out of 10 attempts.
    b. 7 successful serves out of 10 attempts.
    c. 6 successful serves out of 10 tries.
    d. 5 or fewer successful serves out of 10 efforts.
17. When passing a free ball, I make ___ perfect passes to the target area out of 10 attempts.
    a. 9
    b. 8
    c. 7
    d. 6 or fewer
18. When receiving serve, I make ____ passes to the target area out of 10 receptions.
    a. 8
    b. 7
    c. 6
    d. 5 or fewer
19. When blocking an opponent's spike, I am successful ___ times out of 10.
    a. 4
    b. 3
    c. 2
    d. 1 or 0
20. When spiking, I successfully place the ball into the opponent's court ___ times out of 10 tries.
    a. 8
    b. 7
    c. 5 or 6
    d. 4 or fewer

Choice a is always the best selection, and choice d is the least preferred. After you have completed the 20 items, calculate your total score by awarding yourself 3 points for every a selected, 2 points for every b, 1 point for every c, and 0 points for each d. Your final score is the total number of points. Your overall rating is then figured by the following scale:

50-60 points = Excellent player
40-49 points = Very good player, but there's still room for improvement
30-39 points = Good player—keep practicing
20-29 points = Weak player, with *lots* of room for improvement
19 points or less = Need to return to learning the basics

Player Evaluation

Now ask your teacher, coach, or a trained partner to watch you perform at least three times. The evaluator should record your game responses on the scoresheet below.

Game Scoresheet

Name_____

Place a tally mark by the skill the player performs within a game situation. Add a slash mark across the tally mark if the student was also accurate. In the last column, total the scores for all three dates.

For example, say the player serves six times in a game. If four of those serves land in the opponent's court, then the tally marks would look like this: + + + + | |.

Skill	Date	Date	Date	Total ____ of ____
Serve			/	
Pass				
Set				
Attack				
a. Tip				
b. Off-Speed				
c. Hard-Driven Spike				
Block				
Dig				
Individual Defense				
a. Roll				
b. Sprawl				

SUGGESTED RESOURCES

Books

Beal, D., Peppler, M.J., & Kessel, L. (1990). *Coaching tips for the 90's.* Evanston, IL: The Sports Group.

Bertucci, B. & Paterson, J. (1992). *Volleyball drill book: Individual skills.* Indianapolis: Masters Press.

Dougherty, N.J. (Ed.) (1993). *Principles of safety in physical education and sport.* Reston, VA: American Alliance for Health, Physical Education, Recreation and Dance.

Dougherty, N.J. (Ed.) (1993). *Physical education and sport for the secondary school student.* Reston, VA: American Alliance for Health, Physical Education, Recreation and Dance.

Fraser, S.D. (1988). *Strategies for competitive volleyball.* Champaign, IL: Leisure Press.

Hebert, M. (1991). *Insights and strategies for winning volleyball.* Champaign, IL: Leisure Press.

McGown, C. (Ed.) (1994). *Science of coaching volleyball.* Champaign, IL: Human Kinetics.

Neville, W. (1994). *Serve it up.* Mountain View, CA: Mayfield Publishing.

Neville, W. (1990). *Coaching volleyball successfully.* Champaign, IL: Leisure Press.

Scates, A.E. (1988). *Winning volleyball* (3rd ed.). Dubuque, IA: Wm. C. Brown.

Stokes, R., & Haley, M. (1992). *Volleyball everyone.* Winston-Salem, NC: Hunter Textbooks.

Periodicals

Coaching Volleyball is the official technical journal of the American Volleyball Coaches Association. It is published six times a year (October, December, February, April, June, and August). *Coaching Volleyball* is a membership benefit of the AVCA.

Videos

Championship Books and Video Productions: Ames, IA.

DeBoer, *Attacking.*

DeBoer, *Individual defense.*

Dunning, *Team drills.*

Dunning, *Training a setter.*

Gimmillaro, *Defense and passing drills.*

Gimmillaro, *Jump, quickness and conditioning drills.*

Gimmillaro, *Spiking: Step by step development.*

Haley, *Texas team defense.*

Hebert, *Quick and combination attack.*

Mealer, *Team offensive systems.*

Pettit, *Serving and serving strategy.*

Shaw, *Blocking.*

Shaw, *Passing.*

CD-ROM

The interactive guide to volleyball (1994). Renton, WA: Sisu Software.

ABOUT THE AUTHORS

Bonnie Jill Ferguson   **Barbara L. Viera**

Barbara L. Viera has coached and taught volleyball at all levels for more than 30 years. She is a professor of physical education and the head volleyball coach at the University of Delaware.

Barbara's teams at Delaware have competed successfully at the Division I level, achieving a win/loss record that places her in the all-time top 10 of active Division I winning coaches in the country. Her teams have won more than 600 college matches, and Barbara has been selected three times as Conference Coach of the Year. Barbara also has established a successful junior volleyball program for high school and junior high school players in Delaware and continues to serve on its executive committee.

The author of several articles and chapters in books, journals, and newsletters, Barbara has made presentations at regional, national, and international conferences. She has taught volleyball in Argentina, Barbados, Costa Rica, Guatemala, Panama, and Mexico, working with teachers, coaches, national teams, and players of all ages. Her teams have competed in St. Lucia and Barbados.

Bonnie Jill Ferguson is an associate professor of physical education and the head coach of the women's softball team at the University of Delaware. In addition, she is the NCAA Compliance Coordinator.

For more than 14 years, BJ's responsibilities have included teaching the skills, techniques, and analysis of volleyball to students preparing to be physical education teachers. Together, BJ and Barbara have established a competency-based model for teaching volleyball. Through five years of competitive playing experience at the collegiate and United States Volleyball Association levels, BJ developed a unique perspective on volleyball, giving her insight into the various aspects of the game from a player's point of view.